Collected Shorter Poems
1927-1957

By W. H. Auden

ON THIS ISLAND

POEMS

ANOTHER TIME

THE DOUBLE MAN

LETTERS FROM ICELAND
(with Louis MacNeice)

JOURNEY TO A WAR
(with Christopher Isherwood)

THE DOG BENEATH THE SKIN (a play)
(with Christopher Isherwood)

THE ASCENT OF F-6 (a play)
(with Christopher Isherwood)

ON THE FRONTIER (a play)
(with Christopher Isherwood)

FOR THE TIME BEING

THE COLLECTED POETRY OF W. H. AUDEN

THE SELECTED POETRY OF W. H. AUDEN
(Modern Library)

THE AGE OF ANXIETY

NONES

THE ENCHAFÈD FLOOD (three essays)
(Vintage Books)

THE SHIELD OF ACHILLES

THE MAGIC FLUTE (a libretto)
(with Chester Kallman)

HOMAGE TO CLIO

THE DYER'S HAND (essays)

ABOUT THE HOUSE

THE ORATORS

COLLECTED SHORTER POEMS

W. H. Auden, *Wystan Hugh* *1907-* *Collected*

Shorter

Poems

1927-1957

Random House, NEW YORK

PR
6001
.U4
A17
1967

FIRST PRINTING

For
CHRISTOPHER ISHERWOOD
and
CHESTER KALLMAN

Although you be, as I am, one of those
Who feel a Christian ought to write in prose,
For poetry is magic: born in sin, you
May read it to exorcise the Gentile in you.

Contents

9

PART TWO
(1933—1938)

PART THREE
(1939—1947)

PART FOUR
(1948—1957)

Foreword

IN 1944, when I first assembled my shorter pieces, I arranged them in the alphabetical order of their first lines. This may have been a silly thing to do, but I had a reason. At the age of thirty-seven I was still too young to have any sure sense of the direction in which I was moving, and I did not wish critics to waste their time, and mislead readers, making guesses about it which would almost certainly turn out to be wrong. To-day, nearing sixty, I believe that I know myself and my poetic intentions better and, if anybody wants to look at my writings from an historical perspective, I have no objection. Consequently, though I have sometimes shuffled poems so as to bring together those related by theme or genre, in the main their order is chronological.

Some poems which I wrote and, unfortunately, published, I have thrown out because they were dishonest, or bad-mannered, or boring.

A dishonest poem is one which expresses, no matter how well, feelings or beliefs which its author never felt or entertained. For example, I once expressed a desire for 'New styles of architecture'; but I have never liked modern architecture. I prefer *old* styles, and one must be honest even about one's prejudices. Again, and much more shamefully, I once wrote:

> History to the defeated
> may say alas but cannot help nor pardon.

To say this is to equate goodness with success. It would have been bad enough if I had ever held this wicked doctrine, but that I should have stated it simply because it sounded to me rhetorically effective is quite inexcusable.

In art as in life, bad manners, not to be confused with a deliberate intention to cause offence, are the consequence of an over-concern with one's own ego and a lack of consideration for (and knowledge of) others. Readers, like friends, must not be shouted at or treated with brash familiarity. Youth may be forgiven when it is brash or noisy, but this does not mean that brashness and noise are virtues.

Boredom is a subjective reaction but, if a poem makes its author yawn, he can hardly expect a less partial reader to wade through it.

A good many of the poems have been revised. Critics, I have observed, are apt to find revisions ideologically significant. One, even, made a great to-do about what was in fact a typographical error. I can only say that I have never, consciously at any rate, attempted to revise my former thoughts or feelings, only the language in which they were first expressed when, on further consideration, it seemed to me inaccurate, lifeless, prolix or painful to the ear. Re-reading my poems, I find that in the nineteen-thirties I fell into some very slovenly verbal habits. The definite article is always a headache to any poet writing in English, but my addiction to German usages became a disease. Again, it makes me wince when I see how ready I was to treat -*or* and -*aw* as homophones. It is true that in the Oxonian dialect I speak they are, but that isn't really an adequate excuse. I also find that my ear will no longer tolerate rhyming a voiced *S* with an unvoiced. I have had to leave a few such rhymes because I cannot at the moment see a way to get rid of them, but I promise not to do it again. On revisions as a matter of principle, I agree with Valéry: 'A poem is never finished; it is only abandoned.'

This collection stops at the year nineteen-fifty-seven. In the following year I transferred my summer residence from Italy to Austria, so starting a new chapter in my life which is not yet finished. The poems included cover a span of thirty years, there are, if I've counted rightly, three hundred of them, I was twenty when I wrote the earliest, fifty when I wrote the latest: four nice round numbers. Besides, the volume looks alarmingly big already.

W.H.A.

Part I
1927-1932

The Letter

From the very first coming down
Into a new valley with a frown
Because of the sun and a lost way,
You certainly remain: to-day
I, crouching behind a sheep-pen, heard
Travel across a sudden bird,
Cry out against the storm, and found
The year's arc a completed round
And love's worn circuit re-begun,
Endless with no dissenting turn.
Shall see, shall pass, as we have seen
The swallow on the tile, spring's green
Preliminary shiver, passed
A solitary truck, the last
Of shunting in the Autumn. But now,
To interrupt the homely brow,
Thought warmed to evening through and through
Your letter comes, speaking as you,
Speaking of much but not to come.

Nor speech is close nor fingers numb,
If love not seldom has received
An unjust answer, was deceived.
I, decent with the seasons, move
Different or with a different love,
Nor question overmuch the nod,
The stone smile of this country god
That never was more reticent,
Always afraid to say more than it meant.

Taller To-day

Taller to-day, we remember similar evenings,
Walking together in a windless orchard
Where the brook runs over the gravel, far from the glacier.

Nights come bringing the snow, and the dead howl
Under headlands in their windy dwelling
Because the Adversary put too easy questions
On lonely roads.

But happy now, though no nearer each other,
We see farms lighted all along the valley;
Down at the mill-shed hammering stops
And men go home.

Noises at dawn will bring
Freedom for some, but not this peace
No bird can contradict: passing but here, sufficient now
For something fulfilled this hour, loved or endured.

Missing

From scars where kestrels hover,
The leader looking over
Into the happy valley,
Orchard and curving river,
May turn away to see
The slow fastidious line
That disciplines the fell,
Hear curlew's creaking call
From angles unforeseen,
The drumming of a snipe
Surprise where driven sleet
Had scalded to the bone
And streams are acrid yet
To an unaccustomed lip;

The tall unwounded leader
Of doomed companions, all
Whose voices in the rock
Are now perpetual,
Fighters for no one's sake,
Who died beyond the border.

Heroes are buried who
Did not believe in death,
And bravery is now,
Not in the dying breath
But resisting the temptations
To skyline operations.
Yet glory is not new;
The summer visitors
Still come from far and wide,
Choosing their spots to view
The prize competitors,
Each thinking that he will
Find heroes in the wood,
Far from the capital,
Where lights and wine are set
For supper by the lake,
But leaders must migrate:
'Leave for Cape Wrath to-night,'
And the host after waiting
Must quench the lamps and pass
Alive into the house.

The Secret Agent

Control of the passes was, he saw, the key
To this new district, but who would get it?
He, the trained spy, had walked into the trap
For a bogus guide, seduced by the old tricks.

At Greenhearth was a fine site for a dam
And easy power, had they pushed the rail
Some stations nearer. They ignored his wires:
The bridges were unbuilt and trouble coming.

The street music seemed gracious now to one
For weeks up in the desert. Woken by water
Running away in the dark, he often had
Reproached the night for a companion
Dreamed of already. They would shoot, of course,
Parting easily two that were never joined.

The Watershed

Who stands, the crux left of the watershed,
On the wet road between the chafing grass
Below him sees dismantled washing-floors,
Snatches of tramline running to a wood,
An industry already comatose,
Yet sparsely living. A ramshackle engine
At Cashwell raises water; for ten years
It lay in flooded workings until this,
Its latter office, grudgingly performed.
And, further, here and there, though many dead
Lie under the poor soil, some acts are chosen
Taken from recent winters; two there were
Cleaned out a damaged shaft by hand, clutching
The winch a gale would tear them from; one died
During a storm, the fells impassable,
Not at his village, but in wooden shape
Through long abandoned levels nosed his way
And in his final valley went to ground.

Go home, now, stranger, proud of your young stock,
Stranger, turn back again, frustrate and vexed:
This land, cut off, will not communicate,
Be no accessory content to one
Aimless for faces rather there than here.
Beams from your car may cross a bedroom wall,
They wake no sleeper; you may hear the wind
Arriving driven from the ignorant sea
To hurt itself on pane, on bark of elm
Where sap unbaffled rises, being spring;
But seldom this. Near you, taller than grass,
Ears poise before decision, scenting danger.

No Change of Place

Who will endure
Heat of day and winter danger,
Journey from one place to another,
Nor be content to lie
Till evening upon headland over bay,
Between the land and sea
Or smoking wait till hour of food,
Leaning on chained-up gate
At edge of wood?

Metals run,
Burnished or rusty in the sun,
From town to town,
And signals all along are down;
Yet nothing passes
But envelopes between these places,
Snatched at the gate and panting read indoors,
And first spring flowers arriving smashed,
Disaster stammered over wires,
And pity flashed.

For should professional traveller come,
Asked at the fireside, he is dumb,

Declining with a secret smile,
And all the while
Conjectures on our maps grow stranger
And threaten danger.

There is no change of place:
No one will ever know
For what conversion brilliant capital is waiting,
What ugly feast may village band be celebrating;
For no one goes
Further than railhead or the ends of piers,
Will neither go nor send his son
Further through foothills than the rotting stack
Where gaitered gamekeeper with dog and gun
Will shout 'Turn back'.

Let History Be My Judge

We made all possible preparations,
Drew up a list of firms,
Constantly revised our calculations
And allotted the farms,

Issued all the orders expedient
In this kind of case:
Most, as was expected, were obedient,
Though there were murmurs, of course;

Chiefly against our exercising
Our old right to abuse:
Even some sort of attempt at rising,
But these were mere boys.

For never serious misgiving
Occurred to anyone,
Since there could be no question of living
If we did not win.

The generally accepted view teaches
That there was no excuse,
Though in the light of recent researches
Many would find the cause

In a not uncommon form of terror;
Others, still more astute,
Point to possibilities of error
At the very start.

As for ourselves there is left remaining
Our honour at least,
And a reasonable chance of retaining
Our faculties to the last.

Never Stronger

Again in conversations
Speaking of fear
And throwing off reserve
The voice is nearer
But no clearer
Than first love
Than boys' imaginations.

For every news
Means pairing off in twos and twos,
Another I, another You,
Each knowing what to do
But of no use.

Never stronger
But younger and younger,
Saying good-bye but coming back, for fear
Is over there,
And the centre of anger
Is out of danger.

This Loved One

Before this loved one
Was that one and that one,
A family
And history
And ghost's adversity,
Whose pleasing name
Was neighbourly shame.
Before this last one
Was much to be done,
Frontiers to cross
As clothes grew worse,
And coins to pass
In a cheaper house,
Before this last one,
Before this loved one.

Face that the sun
Is lively on
May stir but here
Is no new year;
This gratitude for gifts is less
Than the old loss,
Touching a shaking hands
On mortgaged lands,
And smiling of
This gracious greeting,
'Good day. Good luck',
Is no real meeting,
But instinctive look,
A backward love.

Easy Knowledge

Between attention and attention,
The first and last decision,
Is mortal distraction
Of earth and air,
Further and nearer,
The vague wants
Of days and nights,
And personal error;
And the fatigued face,
Taking the strain
Of the horizontal force
And the vertical thrust,
Makes random answer
To the crucial test;
The uncertain flesh,
Scraping back chair
For the wrong train,
Falling in slush
Before a friend's friends
Or shaking hands
With a snub-nosed winner.

The opening window, closing door,
Open, close, but not
To finish or restore;
These wishes get
No further than
The edges of the town,
And leaning asking from the car
Cannot tell us where we are;
While the divided face
Has no grace
No discretion,
No occupation
But registering
Acreage, mileage,
Of the virtuous thing.

Too Dear, Too Vague

Love by ambition
Of definition
Suffers partition
And cannot go
From yes to no,
For no is not love; no is no,
The shutting of a door,
The tightening jaw,
A wilful sorrow;
And saying yes
Turns love into success,
Views from the rail
Of land and happiness;
Assured of all,
The sofas creak,
And were this all, love were
But cheek to cheek
And dear to dear.

Voices explain
Love's pleasure and love's pain,
Still tap the knee
And cannot disagree,
Hushed for aggression
Of full confession,
Likeness to likeness
Of each old weakness;
Love is not there,
Love has moved to another chair,
Aware already
Of what stands next,
And is not vexed,
And is not giddy,
Leaves the North in place
With a good grace,
And would not gather
Another to another,

Designs his own unhappiness
Foretells his own death and is faithless.

Between Adventure

Upon this line between adventure
Prolong the meeting out of good nature
Obvious in each agreeable feature.

Calling of each other by name,
Smiling, taking a willing arm,
Has the companionship of a game.

But should the walk do more than this
Out of bravado or drunkenness,
Forward or back are menaces.

On neither side let foot slip over,
Invading Always, exploring Never,
For this is hate and this is fear.

On narrowness stand, for sunlight is
Brightest only on surfaces;
No anger, no traitor, but peace.

A Free One

Watch any day his nonchalant pauses, see
His dextrous handling of a wrap as he
Steps after into cars, the beggar's envy.

'There is a free one,' many say, but err.
He is not that returning conqueror,
Nor ever the poles' circumnavigator.

But poised between shocking falls on razor-edge
Has taught himself this balancing subterfuge
Of an accosting profile, an erect carriage.

The song, the varied action of the blood,
Would drown the warning from the iron wood,
Would cancel the inertia of the buried:

Travelling by daylight on from house to house
The longest way to an intrinsic peace,
With love's fidelity and with love's weakness.

Family Ghosts

The strings' excitement, the applauding drum,
Are but the initiating ceremony
That out of cloud the ancestral face may come,

And never hear their subaltern mockery,
Graffiti-writers, moss-grown with whimsies,
Loquacious when the watercourse is dry.

It is your face I see, and morning's praise
Of you is ghost's approval of the choice,
Filtered through roots of the effacing grass.

Fear, taking me aside, would give advice
'To conquer her, the visible enemy,
It is enough to turn away the eyes.'

Yet there's no peace in the assaulted city,
But speeches at the corners, hope for news,
Outside the watchfires of a stronger army.

And all emotions to expression come,
Recovering the archaic imagery:
This longing for assurance takes the form

Of a hawk's vertical stooping from the sky;
These tears, salt for a disobedient dream,
The lunatic agitation of the sea;

While this despair with hardened eyeballs cries
'A Golden Age, a Silver . . . rather this,
Massive and taciturn years, the Age of Ice'.

The Questioner Who Sits So Sly

Will you turn a deaf ear
To what they said on the shore,
Interrogate their poises
In their rich houses;

Of stork-legged heaven-reachers,
Of the compulsory touchers,
The sensitive amusers,
And masked amazers?

Yet wear no ruffian badge,
Nor lie behind the hedge,
Waiting with bombs of conspiracy
In arm-pit secrecy;

Carry no talisman
For germ or the abrupt pain,
Needing no concrete shelter
Nor porcelain filter?

Will you wheel death anywhere
In his invalid chair,
With no affectionate instant
But his attendant?

For to be held as friend
By an undeveloped mind,
To be joke for children is
Death's happiness:

31

Whose anecdotes betray
His favourite colour as blue,
Colour of distant bells
And boy's overalls.

His tales of the bad lands
Disturb the sewing hands;
Hard to be superior
On parting nausea;

To accept the cushions from
Women against martyrdom,
Yet applauding the circuits
Of racing cyclists.

Never to make signs,
Fear neither maelstrom nor zones,
Salute with soldiers' wives
When the flag waves;

Remembering there is
No recognized gift for this;
No income, no bounty,
No promised country.

But to see brave sent home
Hermetically sealed with shame,
And cold's victorious wrestle
With molten metal.

A neutralizing peace
And an average disgrace
Are honour to discover
For later other.

Venus Will Now Say a Few Words

Since you are going to begin to-day
Let us consider what it is you do.
You are the one whose part it is to lean,
For whom it is not good to be alone.
Laugh warmly turning shyly in the hall
Or climb with bare knees the volcanic hill,
Acquire that flick of wrist and after strain
Relax in your darling's arms like a stone,
Remembering everything you can confess,
Making the most of firelight, of hours of fuss;
But joy is mine not yours — to have come so far,
Whose cleverest invention was lately fur;
Lizards my best once who took years to breed,
Could not control the temperature of blood.
To reach that shape for your face to assume,
Pleasure to many and despair to some,
I shifted ranges, lived epochs handicapped
By climate, wars, or what the young men kept,
Modified theories on the types of dross,
Altered desire and history of dress.
You in the town now call the exile fool
That writes home once a year as last leaves fall,
Think — Romans had a language in their day
And ordered roads with it, but it had to die:
Your culture can but leave — forgot as sure
As place-name origins in favourite shire —
Jottings for stories, some often-mentioned Jack,
And references in letters to a private joke,
Equipment rusting in unweeded lanes,
Virtues still advertised on local lines;
And your conviction shall help none to fly,
Cause rather a perversion on next floor.

Nor even is despair your own, when swiftly
Comes general assault on your ideas of safety:
That sense of famine, central anguish felt
For goodness wasted at peripheral fault,

Your shutting up the house and taking prow
To go into the wilderness to pray,
Means that I wish to leave and to pass on,
Select another form, perhaps your son;
Though he reject you, join opposing team
Be late or early at another time,
My treatment will not differ — he will be tipped,
Found weeping, signed for, made to answer, topped.
Do not imagine you can abdicate;
Before you reach the frontier you are caught;
Others have tried it and will try again
To finish that which they did not begin:
Their fate must always be the same as yours,
To suffer the loss they were afraid of, yes,
Holders of one position, wrong for years.

1929

I

It was Easter as I walked in the public gardens,
Hearing the frogs exhaling from the pond,
Watching traffic of magnificent cloud
Moving without anxiety on open sky —
Season when lovers and writers find
An altering speech for altering things,
An emphasis on new names, on the arm
A fresh hand with fresh power.
But thinking so I came at once
Where solitary man sat weeping on a bench,
Hanging his head down, with his mouth distorted
Helpless and ugly as an embryo chicken.

So I remember all of those whose death
Is necessary condition of the season's putting forth,
Who, sorry in this time, look only back
To Christmas intimacy, a winter dialogue
Fading in silence, leaving them in tears.

And recent particulars come to mind;
The death by cancer of a once hated master,
A friend's analysis of his own failure,
Listened to at intervals throughout the winter
At different hours and in different rooms.
But always with success of others for comparison,
The happiness, for instance, of my friend Kurt Groote,
Absence of fear in Gerhart Meyer
From the sea, the truly strong man.

A 'bus ran home then, on the public ground
Lay fallen bicycles like huddled corpses:
No chattering valves of laughter emphasised
Nor the swept gown ends of a gesture stirred
The sessile hush; until a sudden shower
Fell willing into grass and closed the day,
Making choice seem a necessary error.

II

Coming out of me living is always thinking,
Thinking changing and changing living,
Am feeling as it was seeing —
In city leaning on harbour parapet
To watch a colony of duck below
Sit, preen, and doze on buttresses
Or upright paddle on flickering stream,
Casually fishing at a passing straw.
Those find sun's luxury enough,
Shadow know not of homesick foreigner
Nor restlessness of intercepted growth.

All this time was anxiety at night,
Shooting and barricade in street.
Walking home late I listened to a friend
Talking excitedly of final war
Of proletariat against police —
That one shot girl of nineteen through the knees

They threw that one down concrete stair —
Till I was angry, said I was pleased.

Time passes in Hessen, in Gutensberg,
With hill-top and evening holds me up,
Tiny observer of enormous world.
Smoke rises from factory in field,
Memory of fire: On all sides heard
Vanishing music of isolated larks:
From village square voices in hymn,
Men's voices, an old use.
And I above standing, saying in thinking:

'Is first baby, warm in mother,
Before born and is still mother,
Time passes and now is other,
Is knowledge in him now of other,
Cries in cold air, himself no friend.
In grown man also, may see in face,
In his day-thinking and in his night-thinking,
Is wareness and is fear of other,
Alone in flesh, himself no friend.'

He says, 'We must forgive and forget,'
Forgetting saying but is unforgiving
And unforgiving is in his living;
Body reminds in him to loving,
Reminds but takes no further part,
Perfunctorily affectionate in hired room
But takes no part and is unloving
But loving death. May see in dead,
In face of dead that loving wish,
As one returns from Africa to wife
And his ancestral property in Wales.

Yet sometimes men look and say good
At strict beauty of locomotive,
Completeness of gesture or unclouded eye;
In me so absolute unity of evening

And field and distance was in me for peace
Was over me in feeling without forgetting
Those ducks' indifference, that friend's hysteria,
Without wishing and with forgiving,
To love my life, not as other,
Not as bird's life, not as child's,
'Cannot', I said, 'being no child now nor a bird.'

III

Order to stewards and the study of time,
Correct in books, was earlier than this
But joined this by the wires I watched from train,
Slackening of wire and posts' sharp reprimand,
In month of August to a cottage coming.

Being alone, the frightened soul
Returns to this life of sheep and hay
No longer his: he every hour
Moves further from this and must so move,
As child is weaned from his mother and leaves home
But taking the first steps falters, is vexed,
Happy only to find home, a place
Where no tax is levied for being there.

So, insecure, he loves and love
Is insecure, gives less than he expects.
He knows not if it be seed in time to display
Luxuriantly in a wonderful fructification
Or whether it be but a degenerate remnant
Of something immense in the past but now
Surviving only as the infectiousness of disease
Or in the malicious caricature of drunkenness;
Its end glossed over by the careless but known long
To finer perception of the mad and ill.

Moving along the track which is himself,
He loves what he hopes will last, which gone,
Begins the difficult work of mourning,

And as foreign settlers to strange country come,
By mispronunciation of native words
And intermarriage create a new race,
A new language, so may the soul
Be weaned at last to independent delight.

Startled by the violent laugh of a jay
I went from wood, from crunch underfoot,
Air between stems as under water;
As I shall leave the summer, see autumn come
Focusing stars more sharply in the sky,
See frozen buzzard flipped down the weir
And carried out to sea, leave autumn,
See winter, winter for earth and us,
A forethought of death that we may find ourselves at death
Not helplessly strange to the new conditions.

IV

It is time for the destruction of error.
The chairs are being brought in from the garden,
The summer talk stopped on that savage coast
Before the storms, after the guests and birds:
In sanatoriums they laugh less and less,
Less certain of cure; and the loud madman
Sinks now into a more terrible calm.
The falling children know it, the children,
At play on the fuming alkali-tip
Or by the flooded football ground know it —
This is the dragon's day, the devourer's:
Orders are given to the enemy for a time
With underground proliferation of mould,
With constant whisper and with casual question,
To haunt the poisoned in his shunned house,
To destroy the efflorescence of the flesh,
The intricate play of the mind, enforce
Conformity with the orthodox bone.

You whom I gladly walk with, touch,
Or wait for as one certain of good,
We know it, know that love
Needs more than the admiring excitement of union,
More than the abrupt self-confident farewell,
The heel on the finishing blade of grass,
The self-confidence of the falling root,
Needs death, death of the grain, our death,
Death of the old gang; would leave them
In sullen valley where is made no friend,
The old gang to be forgotten in the spring,
The hard bitch and the riding-master,
Stiff underground; deep in clear lake
The lolling bridegroom, beautiful, there.

The Bonfires

Look there! The sunk road winding
To the fortified farm.
Listen! The cock's alarm
In the strange valley.

Are we the stubborn athletes;
Are we then to begin
The run between the gin
And bloody falcon?

The horns of the dark squadron
Converging to attack;
The sound behind our back
Of glaciers calving.

In legend all were simple,
And held the straitened spot;
But we in legend not,
Are not simple.

In weakness how much further;
Along what crooked route
By hedgehog's gradual foot,
Or fish's fathom.

Bitter the blue smoke rises
From garden bonfires lit,
To where we burning sit:
Good, if it's thorough,

Leaving no double traitor
In days of luck and heat,
To time the double beat,
At last together.

On Sunday Walks

On Sunday walks
Past the shut gates of works
The conquerors come
And are handsome.

Sitting all day
By the open window,
Say what they say,
Know what to know,
Who brought and taught
Unusual images
And new tunes to old cottages,
With so much done,
Without a thought
Of the anonymous lampoon,
The cellar counterplot,
Though in the night,
Pursued by eaters,
They clutch at gaiters

That straddle and deny
Escape that way,
Though in the night
Is waking fright.

Father by son
Lives on and on,
Though over date
And motto on the gate
The lichen grows
From year to year,
Still here and there
That Roman nose
Is noticed in the villages,
And father's son
Knows what they said
And what they did.

Not meaning to deceive,
Wish to give suck
Enforces make-believe,
And what was fear
Of fever and bad-luck
Is now a scare
At certain names,
A need for charms,
For certain words
At certain fords,
And what was livelihood
Is tallness, strongness,
Words and longness,
All glory and all story,
Solemn and not so good.

Shorts

Pick a quarrel, go to war,
Leave the hero in the bar;
Hunt the lion, climb the peak:
No one guesses you are weak.

* * *

The friends of the born nurse
Are always getting worse.

* * *

When he is well
She gives him hell,
But she's a brick
When he is sick.

* * *

You're a long way off becoming a saint
So long as you suffer from any complaint;
But, if you don't, there's no denying
The chances are that you're not trying.

* * *

I'm afraid there's many a spectacled sod
Prefers the British Museum to God.

* * *

I'm beginning to lose patience
With my personal relations:
They are not deep,
And they are not cheap.

* * *

Those who will not reason
Perish in the act:
Those who will not act
Perish for that reason.

Let us honour if we can
The vertical man,
Though we value none
But the horizontal one.

* * *

These had stopped seeking
But went on speaking,
Have not contributed
But have diluted.

These ordered light
But had no right,
These handed on
War and a son.

Wishing no harm
But to be warm,
These fell asleep
On the burning heap.

* * *

Private faces in public places
Are wiser and nicer
Than public faces in private places.

Happy Ending

The silly fool, the silly fool
Was sillier in school
But beat the bully as a rule.

The youngest son, the youngest son
Was certainly no wise one
Yet could surprise one.

Or rather, or rather,
To be posh, we gather,
One should have no father.

Simple to prove
That deeds indeed
In life succeed,
But love in love,
And tales in tales
Where no one fails.

This Lunar Beauty

This lunar beauty
Has no history,
Is complete and early;
If beauty later
Bear any feature,
It had a lover
And is another.

This like a dream
Keeps other time,
And daytime is
The loss of this;
For time is inches
And the heart's changes,
Where ghost has haunted
Lost and wanted.

But this was never
A ghost's endeavour
Nor, finished this,
Was ghost at ease;
And till it pass
Love shall not near
The sweetness here,
Nor sorrow take
His endless look.

The Question

To ask the hard question is simple;
Asking at meeting
With the simple glance of acquaintance
To what these go
And how these do:
To ask the hard question is simple,
The simple act of the confused will.

But the answer
Is hard and hard to remember:
On steps or on shore
The ears listening
To words at meeting,
The eyes looking
At the hands helping,
Are never sure
Of what they learn
From how these things are done.
And forgetting to listen or see
Makes forgetting easy;
Only remembering the method of remembering,
Remembering only in another way,
Only the strangely exciting lie,
Afraid
To remember what the fish ignored,
How the bird escaped, or if the sheep obeyed.

Till, losing memory,
Bird, fish, and sheep are ghostly,
And ghosts must do again
What gives them pain.
Cowardice cries
For windy skies,
Coldness for water,
Obedience for a master.

Shall memory restore
The steps and the shore,

The face and the meeting place;
Shall the bird live,
Shall the fish dive,
And sheep obey
In a sheep's way;
Can love remember
The question and the answer,
For love recover
What has been dark and rich and warm all over?

Five Songs

I

What's in your mind, my dove, my coney;
Do thoughts grow like feathers, the dead end of life;
Is it making of love or counting of money,
Or raid on the jewels, the plans of a thief?

Open your eyes, my dearest dallier;
Let hunt with your hands for escaping me;
Go through the motions of exploring the familiar;
Stand on the brink of the warm white day.

Rise with the wind, my great big serpent;
Silence the birds and darken the air;
Change me with terror, alive in a moment;
Strike for the heart and have me there.

II

That night when joy began
Our narrowest veins to flush,
We waited for the flash
Of morning's levelled gun.

But morning let us pass,
And day by day relief
Outgrows his nervous laugh,
Grown credulous of peace,

As mile by mile is seen
No trespasser's reproach,
And love's best glasses reach
No fields but are his own.

III

For what as easy
For what though small,
For what is well
Because between,
To you simply
From me I mean.

Who goes with who
The bedclothes say,
As I and you
Go kissed away,
The data given,
The senses even.

Fate is not late,
Nor the speech rewritten,
Nor one word forgotten,
Said at the start
About heart,
By heart, for heart.

IV

Seen when nights are silent.
The bean-shaped island,
And our ugly comic servant.
Who was observant.

O the veranda and the fruit,
The tiny steamer in the bay
Startling summer with its hoot: —
You have gone away.

V

'O where are you going?' said reader to rider,
'That valley is fatal when furnaces burn,
Yonder's the midden whose odours will madden,
That gap is the grave where the tall return.'

'O do you imagine,' said fearer to farer,
'That dusk will delay on your path to the pass,
Your diligent looking discover the lacking
Your footsteps feel from granite to grass?'

'O what was that bird,' said horror to hearer,
'Did you see that shape in the twisted trees?
Behind you swiftly the figure comes softly,
The spot on your skin is a shocking disease.'

'Out of this house' — said rider to reader,
'Yours never will' — said farer to fearer,
'They're looking for you' — said hearer to horror,
As he left them there, as he left them there.

Uncle Henry

When the Flyin' Scot
fills for shootin', I go southward,
wisin' after coffee, leavin'
Lady Starkie.

Weady for some fun,
visit yearly Wome, Damascus,
in Mowocco look for fwesh a-
-musin' places.

Where I'll find a fwend,
don't you know, a charmin' cweature,
like a Gweek God and devoted:
    how delicious!

All they have they bwing,
Abdul, Nino, Manfwed, Kosta:
here's to women for they bear such
    lovely kiddies!

Consider

Consider this and in our time
As the hawk sees it or the helmeted airman:
The clouds rift suddenly — look there
At cigarette-end smouldering on a border
At the first garden party of the year.
Pass on, admire the view of the massif
Through plate-glass windows of the Sport Hotel;
Join there the insufficient units
Dangerous, easy, in furs, in uniform,
And constellated at reserved tables,
Supplied with feelings by an efficient band,
Relayed elsewhere to farmers and their dogs
Sitting in kitchens in the stormy fens.

Long ago, supreme Antagonist,
More powerful than the great northern whale,
Ancient and sorry at life's limiting defect,
In Cornwall, Mendip, or the Pennine moor
Your comments on the highborn mining-captains,
Found they no answer, made them wish to die
— Lie since in barrows out of harm.
You talk to your admirers every day
By silted harbours, derelict works,
In strangled orchards, and a silent comb
Where dogs have worried or a bird was shot.

Order the ill that they attack at once:
Visit the ports and, interrupting
The leisurely conversation in the bar
Within a stone's throw of the sunlit water,
Beckon your chosen out. Summon
Those handsome and diseased youngsters, those women
Your solitary agents in the country parishes;
And mobilize the powerful forces latent
In soils that make the farmer brutal
In the infected sinus, and the eyes of stoats.
Then, ready, start your rumour, soft
But horrifying in its capacity to disgust
Which, spreading magnified, shall come to be
A polar peril, a prodigious alarm,
Scattering the people, as torn-up paper
Rags and utensils in a sudden gust,
Seized with immeasurable neurotic dread.

Seekers after happiness, all who follow
The convolutions of your simple wish,
It is later than you think; nearer that day
Far other than that distant afternoon
Amid rustle of frocks and stamping feet
They gave the prizes to the ruined boys.
You cannot be away, then, no
Not though you pack to leave within an hour,
Escaping humming down arterial roads:
The date was yours; the prey to fugues,
Irregular breathing and alternate ascendancies
After some haunted migratory years
To disintegrate on an instant in the explosion of mania
Or lapse for ever into a classic fatigue.

The Wanderer

Doom is dark and deeper than any sea-dingle.
Upon what man it fall
In spring, day-wishing flowers appearing,
Avalanche sliding, white snow from rock-face,
That he should leave his house,
No cloud-soft hand can hold him, restraint by women;
But ever that man goes
Through place-keepers, through forest trees,
A stranger to strangers over undried sea,
Houses for fishes, suffocating water,
Or lonely on fell as chat,
By pot-holed becks
A bird stone-haunting, an unquiet bird.

There head falls forward, fatigued at evening,
And dreams of home,
Waving from window, spread of welcome,
Kissing of wife under single sheet;
But waking sees
Bird-flocks nameless to him, through doorway voices
Of new men making another love.

Save him from hostile capture,
From sudden tiger's leap at corner;
Protect his house,
His anxious house where days are counted
From thunderbolt protect,
From gradual ruin spreading like a stain;
Converting number from vague to certain,
Bring joy, bring day of his returning,
Lucky with day approaching, with leaning dawn.

The Watchers

Now from my window-sill I watch the night,
The church clock's yellow face, the green pier light
Burn for a new imprudent year;
The silence buzzes in my ear;
The lights of near-by families are out.

Under the darkness nothing seems to stir;
The lilac bush like a conspirator
Shams dead upon the lawn, and there
Above the flagstaff the Great Bear
Hangs as a portent over Helensburgh.

O Lords of Limit, training dark and light
And setting a tabu 'twixt left and right,
The influential quiet twins
From whom all property begins,
Look leniently upon us all to-night.

No one has seen you: none can say; 'Of late —
Here. You can see the marks — They lay in wait,'
But in my thoughts to-night you seem
Forms which I saw once in a dream,
The stocky keepers of a wild estate.

With guns beneath your arms, in sun and wet,
At doorways posted or on ridges set,
By copse or bridge we know you there
Whose sleepless presences endear
Our peace to us with a perpetual threat.

Look not too closely, be not over-quick;
We have no invitation, but we are sick,
Using the mole's device, the carriage
Of peacock or rat's desperate courage,
And we shall only pass you by a trick.

Deeper towards the summer the year moves on.
What if the starving visionary have seen
The carnival within our gates,
Your bodies kicked about the streets,
We need your power still: use it, that none,

O, from their tables break uncontrollably away,
Lunging, insensible to injury,
Dangerous in a room or out wild–
-ly spinning like a top in the field,
Mopping and mowing through the sleepless day.

Adolescence

By landscape reminded once of his mother's figure
The mountain heights he remembers get bigger and bigger:
With the finest of mapping pens he fondly traces
All the family names on the familiar places.

In a green pasture straying, he walks by still waters;
Surely a swan he seems to earth's unwise daughters,
Bending a beautiful head, worshipping not lying,
'Dear' the dear beak in the dear concha crying.

Under the trees the summer bands were playing;
'Dear boy, be brave as these roots,' he heard them saying:
Carries the good news gladly to a world in danger,
Is ready to argue, he smiles, with any stranger.

And yet this prophet, homing the day is ended,
Receives odd welcome from the country he so defended:
The band roars 'Coward, Coward,' in his human fever,
The giantess shuffles nearer, cries 'Deceiver'.

The Exiles

What siren zooming is sounding our coming
Up frozen fjord forging from freedom,
   What shepherd's call
   When stranded on hill,
   With broken axle
   On track to exile?

With labelled luggage we alight at last,
Joining joking at the junction on the moor,
   With practised smile
   And harmless tale
   Advance to meet
   Each new recruit.

Expert from uplands, always in oilskins,
Recliner from library, laying down law,
   Owner from shire,
   All meet on this shore,
   Facing each prick
   With ginger pluck.

Our rooms are ready, the register signed,
There is time to take a turn before dark,
   See the blistering paint
   On the scorching front,
   Or icicle sombre
   On pierhead timber.

To climb the cliff path to the coastguard's point
Past the derelict dock deserted by rats,
   Look from concrete sill
   Of fort for sale
   To the bathers' rocks,
   The lovers' ricks.

Our boots will be brushed, our bolsters pummelled,
Cupboards are cleared for keeping our clothes:
      Here we shall live
      And somehow love
      Though we only master
      The sad posture.

Picnics are promised and planned for July
To the wood with the waterfall, walks to find,
      Traces of birds,
      A mole, a rivet,
      In factory yards
      Marked strictly private.

There will be skating and curling at Christmas — indoors
Charades and ragging; then riders pass
      Some afternoons
      In snowy lanes,
      Shut in by wires,
      Surplus from wars.

In Spring we shall spade the soil on the border
For blooming of bulbs; we shall bow in Autumn,
      When trees make passes,
      As high gale pushes,
      And bewildered leaves
      Fall on our lives.

Watching through windows the wastes of evening,
The flare of foundries at fall of the year,
      The slight despair
      At what we are,
      The marginal grief
      Is source of life.

In groups forgetting the gun in the drawer
Need pray for no pardon, are proud till recalled
      By music on water
      To lack of stature,
      Saying Alas
      To less and less.

Till holding our hats in our hands for talking,
Or striding down streets for something to see,
     Gas-light in shops,
     The fate of ships,
     And the tide-wind
     Touch the old wound.

Till our nerves are numb and their now is a time
Too late for love or for lying either,
     Grown used at last
     To having lost,
     Accepting dearth,
     The shadow of death.

The Decoys

There are some birds in these valleys
Who flutter round the careless
With intimate appeal,
By seeming kindness trained to snaring,
They feel no falseness.

Under the spell completely
They circle can serenely,
And in the tricky light
The masked hill has a purer greenness.
Their flight looks fleeter.

But fowlers, O, like foxes,
Lie ambushed in the rushes.
Along the harmless tracks
The madman keeper crawls through brushwood,
Axe under oxter.

Alas, the signal given,
Fingers on trigger tighten.
The real unlucky dove
Must smarting fall away from brightness
Its love from living.

Have a Good Time

'We have brought you,' they said, 'a map of the country;
Here is the line that runs to the vats,
This patch of green on the left is the wood,
We've pencilled an arrow to point out the bay.
No thank you, no tea; why look at the clock.
Keep it? Of course. It goes with our love.

We shall watch your future and send our love.
We lived for years, you know, in the country.
Remember at week-ends to wind up the clock.
We've wired to our manager at the vats.
The tides are perfectly safe in the bay,
But whatever you do don't go to the wood.

There's a flying trickster in that wood,
And we shan't be there to help with our love.
Keep fit by bathing in the bay,
You'll never catch fever then in the country.
You're sure of a settled job at the vats
If you keep their hours and live by the clock.'

He arrived at last; it was time by the clock.
He crossed himself as he passed the wood;
Black against evening sky the vats
Brought tears to his eyes as he thought of their love;
Looking out over the darkening country,
He saw the pier in the little bay.

At the week-ends the divers in the bay
Distracted his eyes from the bandstand clock;
When down with fever and in the country
A skein of swans above the wood
Caused him no terror; he came to love
The moss that grew on the derelict vats.

And he has met sketching at the vats
Guests from the new hotel in the bay;

Now, curious, following his love,
His pulses differing from the clock,
Finds consummation in the wood
And sees for the first time the country.

Sees water in the wood and trees by the bay,
Hears a clock striking near the vats;
'This is your country and the home of love'.

Half Way

Having abdicated with comparative ease
And dismissed the greater part of your friends,
Escaping by submarine
In a false beard, half-hoping the ports were watched,
You have got here, and it isn't snowing:
How shall we celebrate your arrival?

Of course we shall mention
Your annual camp for the Tutbury glass-workers,
Your bird-photography phase, your dream at the Hook,
Even your winter in Prague, though not very fully:
Your public refusal of a compass
Is fixed for to-morrow.

Now look at this map.
Red means a first-class, yellow a second-class road,
Crossed swords are for battlefields, gothic characters
For places of archaeological interest.
Our man will drive you as far as the Shot Tower;
Further than that, we fear, is impossible.
At Bigsweir look out for the Kelpie.
If you meet Mr Wren it is wiser to hide.
Consult before leaving a water-doctor.
Do you wish to ask any questions?
                              Good. You may go.

Ode

Though aware of our rank and alert to obey orders,
Watching with binoculars the movement of the grass for an
     ambush,
The pistol cocked, the code-word committed to memory;
          The youngest drummer
Knows all the peace-time stories like the oldest soldier,
          Though frontier-conscious,

About the tall white gods who landed from their open boat,
Skilled in the working of copper, appointing our feast-days,
Before the islands were submerged, when the weather was calm,
          The maned lion common,
An open wishing-well in every garden;
          When love came easy.

Perfectly certain, all of us, but not from the records,
Not from the unshaven agent who returned to the camp:
The pillar dug from the desert recorded only
          The sack of a city,
The agent clutching his side collapsed at our feet,
          'Sorry! They got me!'

Yes, they were living here once but do not now,
Yes, they are living still but do not here;
Lying awake after Lights Out a recruit may speak up:
          'Who told you all this?'
The tent-talk pauses a little till a veteran answers
          'Go to sleep, Sonny!'

Turning over he closes his eyes, and then in a moment
Sees the sun at midnight bright over cornfield and pasture,
Our hope. . . . Someone jostles him, fumbling for boots,
          Time to change guard:
Boy, the quarrel was before your time, the aggressor
          No one you know.

Your childish moments of awareness were all of our world,
At five you sprang, already a tiger in the garden,
At night your mother taught you to pray for our Daddy
        Far away fighting,
One morning you fell off a horse and your brother mocked you:
        'Just like a girl!'

Now we're due to parade on the square in front of the Cathedral,
When the bishop has blessed us, to file in after the choirboys,
To stand with the wine-dark conquerors in the roped-off pews,
        Shout ourselves hoarse:
'They ran like hares; we have broken them up like firewood;
        They fought against God'.

While in a great rift in the limestone miles away
At the same hour they gather, tethering their horses beside them;
A scarecrow prophet from a boulder foresees our judgment,
        Their oppressors howling;
And the bitter psalm is caught by the gale from the rocks:
        'How long shall they flourish?'

What have we all been doing to have made from Fear
That laconic war-bitten captain addressing them now?
Heart and head shall be keener, mood the more
        As our might lessens:
To have caused their shout 'We will fight till we lie down beside
        The Lord we have loved'.

There's Wrath who has learnt every trick of guerrilla warfare,
The shamming dead, the night-raid, the feinted retreat;
Envy their brilliant pamphleteer, to lying
        As husband true,
Expert impersonator and linguist, proud of his power
        To hoodwink sentries.

Gluttony living alone, austerer than us,
Big simple Greed, Acedia famed with them all
For her stamina, keeping the outposts, and somewhere Lust,
        That skilful sapper,

60

Muttering to his fuses in a tunnel 'Could I meet here with Love,
    I would hug her to death'.

There are faces there for which for a very long time
We've been on the look-out, though often at home we imagined
Catching sight of a back or hearing a voice through a doorway
    We had found them at last;
Put our arms round their necks and looked in their eyes
    and discovered
        We were unlucky.

And some of them, surely, we seem to have seen before:
Why, that girl who rode off on her bicycle one fine
    summer evening
And never returned, she's there; and the banker we'd noticed
    Worried for weeks;
Till he failed to arrive one morning and his room was empty,
    Gone with a suitcase.

They speak of things done on the frontier we were never told,
The hidden path to their squat Pictish tower
They will never reveal though kept without sleep, for their
    code is
    'Death to the squealer':
They are brave, yes, though our newspapers mention
    their bravery
    In inverted commas.

But careful; back to our lines; it is unsafe there,
Passports are issued no longer; that area is closed;
There's no fire in the waiting-room now at the climbers'
    Junction,
    And all this year
Work has been stopped on the power-house; the wind
    whistles under
    The half-built culverts.

All leave is cancelled to-night; we must say good-bye.
We entrain at once for the North; we shall see in the morning
The headlands we're doomed to attack; snow down to

the tide-line:
    Though the bunting signals
'Indoors before it's too late; cut peat for your fires,'
    We shall lie out there.

Legend

Enter with him
These legends, Love;
For him assume
Each diverse form,
To legend native,
As legend queer;
That he may do
What these require,
Be, Love, like him
To legend true.

When he to ease
His heart's disease
Must cross in sorrow
Corrosive seas,
As dolphin go;
As cunning fox
Guide through the rocks,
Tell in his ear
The common phrase
Required to please
The guardians there;
And when across
The livid marsh
Big birds pursue,
Again be true,
Between his thighs
As pony rise,
And swift as wind
Bear him away

Till cries and they
Are left behind.

But when at last,
These dangers passed,
His grown desire
Of legend tire,
Then, Love, standing
At legend's ending,
Claim your reward;
Submit your neck
To the ungrateful stroke
Of his reluctant sword,
That, starting back,
His eyes may look
Amazed on you,
Find what he wanted
Is faithful too
But disenchanted,
Love as love.

The Witnesses

Young men late in the night
  Toss on their beds,
Their pillows do not comfort
  Their uneasy heads,
The lot that decides their fate
  Is cast to-morrow,
One must depart and face
  Danger and sorrow.

Is it me? Is it me?

Look in your heart and see:
  There lies the answer.
Though the heart like a clever
  Conjuror or dancer

Deceive you often with many
    A curious sleight,
And motives like stowaways
    Are found too late.

What shall he do, whose heart
    Chooses to depart?

He shall against his peace
    Feel his heart harden,
Envy the heavy birds
    At home in a garden,
For walk he must the empty
    Selfish journey
Between the needless risk
    And the endless safety.

Will he safe and sound
    Return to his own ground?

Clouds and lions stand
    Before him dangerous,
And the hostility of dreams.
    Then let him honour Us,
Lest he should be ashamed
    In the hour of crisis,
In the valley of corrosion
    Tarnish his brightness.

Who are You, whose speech
Sounds far out of reach?

You are the town and We are the clock.
We are the guardians of the gate in the rock,
    The Two.
On your left and on your right,
In the day and in the night,
    We are watching you.

Wiser not to ask just what has occurred
To them who disobeyed our word;
    To those
We were the whirlpool, we were the reef,
We were the formal nightmare, grief
    And the unlucky rose.

Climb up the crane, learn the sailor's words
When the ships from the islands laden with birds
    Come in;
Tell your stories of fishing and other men's wives,
The expansive dreams of constricted lives,
    In the lighted inn.

But do not imagine We do not know,
Or that what you hide with such care won't show
    At a glance:
Nothing is done, nothing is said,
But don't make the mistake of believing us dead;
    I shouldn't dance.

We're afraid in that case you'll have a fall;
We've been watching you over the garden wall
    For hours:
The sky is darkening like a stain;
Something is going to fall like rain,
    And it won't be flowers.

When the green field comes off like a lid,
Revealing what was much better hid—
    Unpleasant:
And look, behind you without a sound
The woods have come up and are standing round
    In deadly crescent.

The bolt is sliding in its groove;
Outside the window is the black remov-
    -er's van:
And now with sudden swift emergence

Come the hooded women, the hump-backed surgeons,
And the Scissor Man.

This might happen any day;
So be careful what you say
And do:
Be clean, be tidy, oil the lock,
Weed the garden, wind the clock;
Remember the Two.

Part II
1933-1938

A Summer Night

(*To Geoffrey Hoyland*)

Out on the lawn I lie in bed,
Vega conspicuous overhead
   In the windless nights of June,
As congregated leaves complete
Their day's activity; my feet
   Point to the rising moon.

Lucky, this point in time and space
Is chosen as my working-place,
   Where the sexy airs of summer,
The bathing hours and the bare arms,
The leisured drives through a land of farms
   Are good to a newcomer.

Equal with colleagues in a ring
I sit on each calm evening
   Enchanted as the flowers
The opening light draws out of hiding
With all its gradual dove-like pleading,
   Its logic and its powers:

That later we, though parted then,
May still recall these evenings when
   Fear gave his watch no look;
The lion griefs loped from the shade
And on our knees their muzzles laid,
   And Death put down his book.

Now north and south and east and west
Those I love lie down to rest;
    The moon looks on them all,
The healers and the brilliant talkers
The eccentrics and the silent walkers,
    The dumpy and the tall.

She climbs the European sky,
Churches and power-stations lie
    Alike among earth's fixtures:
Into the galleries she peers
And blankly as a butcher stares
    Upon the marvellous pictures.

To gravity attentive, she
Can notice nothing here, though we
    Whom hunger does not move,
From gardens where we feel secure
Look up and with a sigh endure
    The tyrannies of love:

And, gentle, do not care to know,
Where Poland draws her eastern bow,
    What violence is done,
Nor ask what doubtful act allows
Our freedom in this English house,
    Our picnics in the sun.

Soon, soon, through dykes of our content
The crumpling flood will force a rent
    And, taller than a tree,
Hold sudden death before our eyes
Whose river dreams long hid the size
    And vigours of the sea.

But when the waters make retreat
And through the black mud first the wheat
    In shy green stalks appears,
When stranded monsters gasping lie,

And sounds of riveting terrify
    Their whorled unsubtle ears,

May these delights we dread to lose,
This privacy, need no excuse
    But to that strength belong,
As through a child's rash happy cries
The drowned parental voices rise
    In unlamenting song.

After discharges of alarm
All unpredicted let them calm
    The pulse of nervous nations,
Forgive the murderer in his glass,
Tough in their patience to surpass
    The tigress her swift motions.

Paysage Moralisé

Hearing of harvests rotting in the valleys,
Seeing at end of street the barren mountains,
Round corners coming suddenly on water,
Knowing them shipwrecked who were launched for islands,
We honour founders of these starving cities
Whose honour is the image of our sorrow,

Which cannot see its likeness in their sorrow
That brought them desperate to the brink of valleys;
Dreaming of evening walks through learned cities
They reined their violent horses on the mountains,
Those fields like ships to castaways on islands,
Visions of green to them who craved for water.

They built by rivers and at night the water
Running past windows comforted their sorrow;
Each in his little bed conceived of islands
Where every day was dancing in the valleys

71

And all the green trees blossomed on the mountains,
Where love was innocent, being far from cities.

But dawn came back and they were still in cities;
No marvellous creature rose up from the water;
There was still gold and silver in the mountains
But hunger was a more immediate sorrow,
Although to moping villages in valleys
Some waving pilgrims were describing islands . . .

'The gods,' they promised, 'visit us from islands,
Are stalking, head-up, lovely, through our cities;
Now is the time to leave your wretched valleys
And sail with them across the lime-green water,
Sitting at their white sides, forget your sorrow,
The shadow cast across your lives by mountains.'

So many, doubtful, perished in the mountains,
Climbing up crags to get a view of islands,
So many, fearful, took with them their sorrow
Which stayed them when they reached unhappy cities,
So many, careless, dived and drowned in water,
So many, wretched, would not leave their valleys.

It is our sorrow. Shall it melt? Then water
Would gush, flush, green these mountains and these valleys,
And we rebuild our cities, not dream of islands.

O What is that Sound

O what is that sound which so thrills the ear
   Down in the valley drumming, drumming?
Only the scarlet soldiers, dear,
   The soldiers coming.

O what is that light I see flashing so clear
   Over the distance brightly, brightly?
Only the sun on their weapons, dear,
   As they step lightly.

O what are they doing with all that gear,
   What are they doing this morning, this morning?
Only their usual manoeuvres, dear,
   Or perhaps a warning.

O why have they left the road down there,
   Why are they suddenly wheeling, wheeling?
Perhaps a change in their orders, dear.
   Why are you kneeling?

O haven't they stopped for the doctor's care,
   Haven't they reined their horses, their horses?
Why, they are none of them wounded, dear,
   None of these forces.

O is it the parson they want, with white hair,
   Is it the parson, is it, is it?
No, they are passing his gateway, dear,
   Without a visit.

O it must be the farmer who lives so near.
   It must be the farmer so cunning, so cunning?
They have passed the farmyard already, dear,
   And now they are running.

O where are you going? Stay with me here!
   Were the vows you swore deceiving, deceiving?
No, I promised to love you, dear,
   But I must be leaving.

O it's broken the lock and splintered the door,
   O it's the gate where they're turning, turning;
Their boots are heavy on the floor
   And their eyes are burning.

Our Hunting Fathers

Our hunting fathers told the story
  Of the sadness of the creatures,
Pitied the limits and the lack
  Set in their finished features;
Saw in the lion's intolerant look,
Behind the quarry's dying glare,
Love raging for the personal glory
  That reason's gift would add,
The liberal appetite and power,
  The rightness of a god.

Who, nurtured in that fine tradition,
  Predicted the result,
Guessed Love by nature suited to
  The intricate ways of guilt,
That human ligaments could so
His southern gestures modify
And make it his mature ambition
  To think no thought but ours,
To hunger, work illegally,
  And be anonymous?

Through the Looking-Glass

Earth has turned over; our side feels the cold,
And life sinks choking in the wells of trees,
A faint heart here and there stops ticking, killed,
Icing on ponds entrances village boys:
Among wreathed holly and wrapped gifts I move,
Old carols on the piano, a glowing hearth,
All our traditional sympathy with birth,
Put by your challenge to the shifts of love.

Your portrait hangs before me on the wall,
And there what view I wish for I shall find,

The wooded or the stony, though not all
The painter's gifts can make its flatness round;
Through each blue iris greet the heaven of failures,
That mirror world where Logic is reversed,
Where age becomes the handsome child at last,
The glass wave parted for the country sailors.

There move the enormous comics, drawn from life —
My father as an Airedale and a gardener,
My mother chasing letters with a knife.
You are not present as a character;
(Only the family have speaking parts).
You are a valley or a river-bend,
The one an aunt refers to as a friend,
The tree from which the weasel racing starts.

Behind me roars that other world it matches,
Love's daytime kingdom which I say you rule,
His total state where all must wear your badges,
Keep order perfect as a naval school.
Noble emotions, organized and massed,
Line the straight flood-lit tracks of memory
To cheer your image as it flashes by,
All lust at once informed on and suppressed.

Yours is the only name expressive there,
And family affection speaks in cypher.
Lay-out of hospital and street and square
That comfort to its homesick children offer,
As I, their author, stand between these dreams,
Unable to choose either for a home,
Your would-be lover who has never come
In a great bed at midnight to your arms.

Such dreams are amorous; they are indeed:
But no one but myself is loved in these,
While time flies on above the dreamer's head,
Flies on, flies on, and with your beauty flies,
And pride succeeds to each succeeding state,

Still able to buy up the life within,
License no liberty except his own,
Order the fireworks after the defeat.

Language of moderation cannot hide: —
My sea is empty and its waves are rough;
Gone from the map the shore where childhood played,
Tight-fisted as a peasant, eating love;
Lost in my wake the archipelago,
Islands of self through which I sailed all day
Planting a pirate's flag, a generous boy;
And lost my way to action and to you.

Lost if I steer. Tempest and tide may blow
Sailor and ship past the illusive reef,
And I yet land to celebrate with you
The birth of natural order and true love:
With you enjoy the untransfigured scene,
My father down the garden in his gaiters,
My mother at her bureau writing letters,
Free to our favours, all our titles gone.

Two Climbs

Fleeing from short-haired mad executives,
The sad and useless faces round my home,
Upon the mountains of my fear I climb:
Above, a breakneck scorching rock; no caves,
No col, no water. With excuse concocted,
Soon on a lower alp I fall and pant,
Cooling my weariness in faults that flaunt
A life which they have stolen and perfected.

Climbing with you was easy as a vow.
We reached the top not hungry in the least,
But it was eyes we looked at, not the view,
Saw nothing but ourselves, left-handed, lost,
Returned to shore, the rich interior still
Unknown: love gave the power, but took the will.

Meiosis

Love had him fast but though he fought for breath
He struggled only to possess Another,
The snare forgotten in their little death,
Till you, the seed to which he was a mother,
That never heard of love, through love was free,
While he within his arms a world was holding,
To take the all-night journey under sea,
Work west and northward, set up building.

Cities and years constricted to your scope,
All sorrow simplified though almost all
Shall be as subtle when you are as tall:
Yet clearly in that 'almost' all his hope
That hopeful falsehood cannot stem with love
The flood on which all move and wish to move.

A Misunderstanding

Just as his dream foretold, he met them all:
The smiling grimy boy at the garage
Ran out before he blew his horn; the tall
Professor in the mountains with his large
Tweed pockets full of plants addressed him hours
Before he would have dared; the deaf girl too
Seemed to expect him at her green chateau;
A meal was laid, the guest-room full of flowers.

More, their talk always took the wished-for turn,
Dwelt on the need for someone to advise,
Yet, at each meeting, he was forced to learn
The same misunderstanding would arise.
Which was in need of help? Were they or he
The physician, bridegroom and incendiary?

Who's Who

A shilling life will give you all the facts:
How Father beat him, how he ran away,
What were the struggles of his youth, what acts
Made him the greatest figure of his day:
Of how he fought, fished, hunted, worked all night,
Though giddy, climbed new mountains; named a sea:
Some of the last researchers even write
Love made him weep his pints like you and me.

With all his honours on, he sighed for one
Who, say astonished critics, lived at home;
Did little jobs about the house with skill
And nothing else; could whistle; would sit still
Or potter round the garden; answered some
Of his long marvellous letters but kept none.

Schoolchildren

Here are all the captivities, the cells are as real,
but these are unlike the prisoners we know,
who are outraged or pining or wittily resigned
    or just wish all away.

For these dissent so little, so nearly content
with the dumb play of dogs, with licking and rushing;
the bars of love are so strong, their conspiracies
    weak like the vows of drunkards.

Indeed, their strangeness is difficult to watch:
the condemned see only the fallacious angels of a vision,
so little effort lies behind their smiling,
    the beast of vocation is afraid.

But watch them, set against our size and timing
their almost neuter, their slightly awkward perfection;
for the sex is there, the broken bootlace is broken:
    the professor's dream is not true.

Yet the tyranny is so easy. An improper word
scribbled upon a fountain, is that all the rebellion?
A storm of tears wept in a corner, are these
    the seeds of a new life?

May

May with its light behaving
Stirs vessel, eye and limb,
The singular and sad
Are willing to recover,
And to each swan-delighting river
The careless picnics come
In living white and red.

Our dead, remote and hooded,
In hollows rest, but we
From their vague woods have broken,
Forests where children meet
And the white angel-vampires flit,
Stand now with shaded eye,
The dangerous apple taken.

The real world lies before us,
Brave motions of the young,
Abundant wish for death,
The pleasing, pleasured, haunted:
A dying Master sinks tormented
In his admirers' ring,
The unjust walk the earth.

And love that makes impatient
Tortoise and roe, that lays
The blonde beside the dark,
Urges upon our blood,
Before the evil and the good
How insufficient is
Touch, endearment, look.

A Bride in the 30's

Easily you move, easily your head,
And easily, as through leaves of an album, I'm led
Through the night's delights and the day's impressions,
Past tenement, river, upland, wood,
Though sombre the sixteen skies of Europe
    And the Danube flood.

Looking and loving, our behaviours pass
Things of stone, of steel and of polished glass;
Lucky to Love the strategic railway,
The run-down farms where his looks are fed,
And in each policed unlucky city
    Lucky his bed.

He from these lands of terrifying mottoes
Makes worlds as innocent as Beatrix Potter's;
Through bankrupt countries where they mend the roads,
Along unending plains his will is,
Intent as a collector, to pursue
    His greens and lilies.

Easy for him to find in your face
A pool of silence or a tower of grace,
To conjure a camera into a wishing-rose,
Simple to excite in the air from a glance
Horses, fountains, a side-drum, a trombone,
    The cosmic dance.

Summoned by such a music from our time,
Such images to sight and audience come
As Vanity cannot dispel or bless,
Hunger and fear in their variations,
Grouped invalids watching movements of birds,
    And single assassins,

Ten desperate million marching by,
Five feet, six feet, seven feet high,
Hitler and Mussolini in their wooing poses,
Churchill acknowledging the voters' greeting,
Roosevelt at the microphone, van der Lubbe laughing,
    And our first meeting.

But Love except at our proposal
Will do no trick at his disposal,
Without opinions of his own performs
The programme that we think of merit,
And through our private stuff must work
    His public spirit.

Certain it became, while still incomplete,
There were prizes for which we would never compete:
A choice was killed by each childish illness,
The boiling tears amid the hot-house plants,
The rigid promise fractured in the garden,
    And the long aunts.

While every day there bolted from the field
Desires to which we could not yield,
Fewer and clearer grew our plans,
Schemes for a life-time, sketches for a hatred,
And early among my interesting scrawls
    Appeared your portrait.

You stand now before me, flesh and bone
That ghosts would like to make their own:
Beware them, look away, be deaf,
When rage would proffer her immediate pleasure
Or glory swap her fascinating rubbish
    For your one treasure.

Be deaf, too, standing uncertain now,
A pine-tree shadow across your brow,
To what I hear and wish I did not,
The voice of Love saying lightly, brightly,
'Be Lubbe, be Hitler, but be my good,
    Daily, nightly.'

Trees are shaken, mountains darken,
But the heart repeats, though we would not hearken:
'Yours the choice to whom the gods awarded
The language of learning, the language of love,
Crooked to move as a money-bug, as a cancer,
    Or straight as a dove.

On This Island

Look, stranger, on this island now
The leaping light for your delight discovers,
Stand stable here
And silent be,
That through the channels of the ear
May wander like a river
The swaying sound of the sea.

Here at the small field's ending pause
When the chalk wall falls to the foam and its tall ledges
Oppose the pluck
And knock of the tide,
And the shingle scrambles after the suck-
-ing surf,
And the gull lodges
A moment on its sheer side.

Far off like floating seeds the ships
Diverge on urgent voluntary errands,
And the full view
Indeed may enter
And move in memory as now these clouds do,
That pass the harbour mirror
And all the summer through the water saunter.

Night Mail

(*Commentary for a G.P.O. Film*)

I

This is the Night Mail crossing the Border,
Bringing the cheque and the postal order,

Letters for the rich, letters for the poor,
The shop at the corner, the girl next door.

Pulling up Beattock, a steady climb:
The gradient's against her, but she's on time.

Past cotton-grass and moorland boulder,
Shovelling white steam over her shoulder,

Snorting noisily, she passes
Silent miles of wind-bent grasses.

Birds turn their heads as she approaches,
Stare from bushes at her blank-faced coaches.

Sheep-dogs cannot turn her course;
They slumber on with paws across.

In the farm she passes no one wakes,
But a jug in a bedroom gently shakes.

II

Dawn freshens. Her climb is done.
Down towards Glasgow she descends,
Towards the steam tugs yelping down a glade of cranes,
Towards the fields of apparatus, the furnaces
Set on the dark plain like gigantic chessmen.
All Scotland waits for her:
In dark glens, beside pale-green lochs,
Men long for news.

III

Letters of thanks, letters from banks,
Letters of joy from girl and boy,
Receipted bills and invitations
To inspect new stock or to visit relations,
And applications for situations,
And timid lovers' declarations,
And gossip, gossip from all the nations,
News circumstantial, news financial,
Letters with holiday snaps to enlarge in,
Letters with faces scrawled on the margin,
Letters from uncles, cousins and aunts,
Letters to Scotland from the South of France,
Letters of condolence to Highlands and Lowlands,
Written on paper of every hue,
The pink, the violet, the white and the blue,
The chatty, the catty, the boring, the adoring,
The cold and official and the heart's outpouring,
Clever, stupid, short and long,
The typed and the printed and the spelt all wrong.

IV

Thousands are still asleep,
Dreaming of terrifying monsters
Or a friendly tea beside the band in Cranston's or Crawford's:
Asleep in working Glasgow, asleep in well-set Edinburgh,
Asleep in granite Aberdeen,
They continue their dreams,
But shall wake soon and hope for letters,
And none will hear the postman's knock
Without a quickening of the heart.
For who can bear to feel himself forgotten?

As I walked out one Evening

As I walked out one evening,
    Walking down Bristol Street,
The crowds upon the pavement
    Were fields of harvest wheat.

And down by the brimming river
    I heard a lover sing
Under an arch of the railway:
    'Love has no ending.

'I'll love you, dear, I'll love you
    Till China and Africa meet,
And the river jumps over the mountain
    And the salmon sing in the street,

'I'll love you till the ocean
    Is folded and hung up to dry
And the seven stars go squawking
    Like geese about the sky.

The years shall run like rabbits,
    For in my arms I hold
The Flower of the Ages,
    And the first love of the world.'

But all the clocks in the city
    Began to whirr and chime:
'O let not Time deceive you,
    You cannot conquer Time.

'In the burrows of the Nightmare
    Where Justice naked is,
Time watches from the shadow
    And coughs when you would kiss.

'In headaches and in worry
  Vaguely life leaks away,
And Time will have his fancy
  To-morrow or to-day.

'Into many a green valley
  Drifts the appalling snow;
Time breaks the threaded dances
  And the diver's brilliant bow.

'O plunge your hands in water,
  Plunge them in up to the wrist;
Stare, stare in the basin
  And wonder what you've missed.

'The glacier knocks in the cupboard,
  The desert sighs in the bed,
And the crack in the tea-cup opens
  A lane to the land of the dead.

'Where the beggars raffle the banknotes
  And the Giant is enchanting to Jack,
And the Lily-white Boy is a Roarer,
  And Jill goes down on her back.

'O look, look in the mirror,
  O look in your distress;
Life remains a blessing
  Although you cannot bless.

'O stand, stand at the window
  As the tears scald and start;
You shall love your crooked neighbour
  With your crooked heart.'

It was late, late in the evening,
  The lovers they were gone;
The clocks had ceased their chiming,
  And the deep river ran on.

Twelve Songs

I

— 'O for doors to be open and an invite with gilded edges
  To dine with Lord Lobcock and Count Asthma on the
     platinum benches,
  With somersaults and fireworks, the roast and the smacking
     kisses' —
       Cried the cripples to the silent statue,
       The six beggared cripples.

— 'And Garbo's and Cleopatra's wits to go astraying,
  In a feather ocean with me to go fishing and playing,
  Still jolly when the cock has burst himself with crowing' —
       Cried the cripples to the silent statue,
       The six beggared cripples.

— 'And to stand on green turf among the craning yellow faces
  Dependent on the chestnut, the sable, and Arabian horses,
  And me with a magic crystal to foresee their places' —
       Cried the cripples to the silent statue.
       The six beggared cripples.

— 'And this square to be a deck and these pigeons canvas to rig,
  And to follow the delicious breeze like a tantony pig
  To the shaded feverless islands where the melons are big' —
       Cried the cripples to the silent statue,
       The six beggared cripples.

— 'And these shops to be turned to tulips in a garden bed,
  And me with my crutch to thrash each merchant dead
  As he pokes from a flower his bald and wicked head' —
       Cried the cripples to the silent statue,
       The six beggared cripples.

— 'And a hole in the bottom of heaven, and Peter and Paul
  And each smug surprised saint like parachutes to fall,
  And every one-legged beggar to have no legs at all' —
       Cried the cripples to the silent statue,
       The six beggared cripples.

II

O lurcher-loving collier, black as night,
Follow your love across the smokeless hill;
Your lamp is out, the cages all are still;
Course for her heart and do not miss,
For Sunday soon is past and, Kate, fly not so fast,
For Monday comes when none may kiss:
Be marble to his soot, and to his black be white.

III

Let a florid music praise,
    The flute and the trumpet,
Beauty's conquest of your face:
In that land of flesh and bone,
Where from citadels on high
Her imperial standards fly,
        Let the hot sun
        Shine on, shine on.

O but the unloved have had power,
    The weeping and striking,
Always: time will bring their hour;
Their secretive children walk
Through your vigilance of breath
To unpardonable Death,
        And my vows break
        Before his look.

IV

Dear, though the night is gone,
Its dream still haunts to-day,
That brought us to a room
Cavernous, lofty as
A railway terminus,
And crowded in that gloom
Were beds, and we in one
In a far corner lay.

Our whisper woke no clocks,
We kissed and I was glad
At everything you did,
Indifferent to those
Who sat with hostile eyes
In pairs on every bed,
Arms round each other's necks,
Inert and vaguely sad.

What hidden worm of guilt
Or what malignant doubt
Am I the victim of,
That you then, unabashed,
Did what I never wished,
Confessed another love;
And I, submissive, felt
Unwanted and went out?

V

Fish in the unruffled lakes
Their swarming colours wear,
Swans in the winter air
A white perfection have,
And the great lion walks
Through his innocent grove;
Lion, fish and swan
Act, and are gone
Upon Time's toppling wave.

We, till shadowed days are done,
We must weep and sing
Duty's conscious wrong,
The Devil in the clock,
The goodness carefully worn
For atonement or for luck;
We must lose our loves,
On each beast and bird that moves
Turn an envious look.

Sighs for folly done and said
Twist our narrow days,
But I must bless, I must praise
That you, my swan, who have
All gifts that to the swan
Impulsive Nature gave,
The majesty and pride,
Last night should add
Your voluntary love.

VI

Now the leaves are falling fast,
Nurse's flowers will not last,
Nurses to their graves are gone,
But the prams go rolling on.

Whispering neighbours left and right
Daunt us from our true delight,
Able hands are left to freeze
Derelict on lonely knees.

Close behind us on our track,
Dead in hundreds cry Alack,
Arms raised stiffly to reprove
In false attitudes of love.

Scrawny through a plundered wood,
Trolls run scolding for their food,
Owl and nightingale are dumb,
And the angel will not come.

Clear, unscaleable, ahead
Rise the Mountains of Instead,
From whose cold cascading streams
None may drink except in dreams.

VII

Underneath an abject willow,
    Lover, sulk no more:
Act from thought should quickly follow.
    What is thinking for?
Your unique and moping station
    Proves you cold;
    Stand up and fold
Your map of desolation.

Bells that toll across the meadows
    From the sombre spire
Toll for these unloving shadows
    Love does not require.
All that lives may love; why longer
    Bow to loss
    With arms across?
Strike and you shall conquer.

Geese in flocks above you flying,
    Their direction know,
Icy brooks beneath you flowing,
    To their ocean go.
Dark and dull is your distraction:
    Walk then, come,
    No longer numb
Into your satisfaction.

VIII

At last the secret is out, as it always must come in the end,
The delicious story is ripe to tell to the intimate friend;
Over the tea-cups and in the square the tongue has its desire;
Still waters run deep, my dear, there's never smoke without
    fire.

Behind the corpse in the reservoir, behind the ghost on the
    links,
Behind the lady who dances and the man who madly drinks,

Under the look of fatigue, the attack of migraine and the sigh
There is always another story, there is more than meets the eye.

For the clear voice suddenly singing, high up in the convent
        wall,
The scent of elder bushes, the sporting prints in the hall,
The croquet matches in summer, the handshake, the cough, the
        kiss,
There is always a wicked secret, a private reason for this.

IX

Stop all the clocks, cut off the telephone,
Prevent the dog from barking with a juicy bone,
Silence the pianos and with muffled drum
Bring out the coffin, let the mourners come.

Let aeroplanes circle moaning overhead
Scribbling on the sky the message He Is Dead,
Put crêpe bows round the white necks of the public doves,
Let the traffic policemen wear black cotton gloves.

He was my North, my South, my East and West,
My working week and my Sunday rest,
My noon, my midnight, my talk, my song;
I thought that love would last for ever: I was wrong.

The stars are not wanted now: put out every one;
Pack up the moon and dismantle the sun;
Pour away the ocean and sweep up the wood.
For nothing now can ever come to any good.

X

O the valley in the summer where I and my John
Beside the deep river would walk on and on
While the flowers at our feet and the birds up above
Argued so sweetly on reciprocal love,
And I leaned on his shoulder; 'O Johnny, let's play':
But he frowned like thunder and he went away.

O that Friday near Christmas as I well recall
When we went to the Charity Matinee Ball,
The floor was so smooth and the band was so loud
And Johnny so handsome I felt so proud;
'Squeeze me tighter, dear Johnny, let's dance till it's day':
But he frowned like thunder and he went away.

Shall I ever forget at the Grand Opera
When music poured out of each wonderful star?
Diamonds and pearls they hung dazzling down
Over each silver or golden silk gown;
'O John I'm in heaven,' I whispered to say:
But he frowned like thunder and he went away.

O but he was as fair as a garden in flower,
As slender and tall as the great Eiffel Tower,
When the waltz throbbed out on the long promenade
O his eyes and his smile they went straight to my heart;
'O marry me, Johnny, I'll love and obey':
But he frowned like thunder and he went away.

O last night I dreamed of you, Johnny, my lover,
You'd the sun on one arm and the moon on the other,
The sea it was blue and the grass it was green,
Every star rattled a round tambourine;
Ten thousand miles deep in a pit there I lay:
But you frowned like thunder and you went away.

XI

Over the heather the wet wind blows,
I've lice in my tunic and a cold in my nose.

The rain comes pattering out of the sky,
I'm a Wall soldier, I don't know why.

The mist creeps over the hard grey stone,
My girl's in Tungria; I sleep alone.

Aulus goes hanging around her place,
I don't like his manners, I don't like his face.

Piso's a Christian, he worships a fish;
There'd be no kissing if he had his wish.

She gave me a ring but I diced it away;
I want my girl and I want my pay.

When I'm a veteran with only one eye
I shall do nothing but look at the sky.

XII

Some say that love's a little boy,
    And some say it's a bird,
Some say it makes the world go round,
    And some say that's absurd,
And when I asked the man next-door,
    Who looked as if he knew,
His wife got very cross indeed,
    And said it wouldn't do.

    Does it look like a pair of pyjamas,
      Or the ham in a temperance hotel?
    Does its odour remind one of llamas,
      Or has it a comforting smell?
    Is it prickly to touch as a hedge is,
      Or soft as eiderdown fluff?
    Is it sharp or quite smooth at the edges?
      O tell me the truth about love.

Our history books refer to it
    In cryptic little notes,
It's quite a common topic on
    The Transatlantic boats;
I've found the subject mentioned in
    Accounts of suicides,
And even seen it scribbled on
    The backs of railway-guides.

Does it howl like a hungry Alsatian,
  Or boom like a military band?
Could one give a first-rate imitation
  On a saw or a Steinway Grand?
Is its singing at parties a riot?
  Does it only like Classical stuff?
Will it stop when one wants to be quiet?
  O tell me the truth about love.

I looked inside the summer-house;
    It wasn't ever there:
I tried the Thames at Maidenhead,
    And Brighton's bracing air.
I don't know what the blackbird sang,
    Or what the tulip said;
But it wasn't in the chicken-run,
    Or underneath the bed.

Can it pull extraordinary faces?
  Is it usually sick on a swing?
Does it spend all its time at the races,
  Or fiddling with pieces of string?
Has it views of its own about money?
  Does it think Patriotism enough?
Are its stories vulgar but funny?
  O tell me the truth about love.

When it comes, will it come without warning
  Just as I'm picking my nose?
Will it knock on my door in the morning,
  Or tread in the bus on my toes?
Will it come like a change in the weather?
  Will its greeting be courteous or rough?
Will it alter my life altogether?
  O tell me the truth about love.

His Excellency

As it is, plenty;
As it's admitted
The children happy,
And the car, the car
That goes so far,
And the wife devoted:
To this as it is,
To the work and the banks
Let his thinning hair
And his hauteur
Give thanks, give thanks.

All that was thought
As like as not is not;
When nothing was enough
But love, but love,
And the rough future
Of an intransigeant nature,
And the betraying smile,
Betraying, but a smile:
That that is not, is not;
Forget, forget.

Let him not cease to praise,
Then, his lordly days;
Yes, and the success
Let him bless, let him bless:
Let him see in this
The profit larger
And the sin venial,
Lest he see as it is
The loss as major
And final, final.

Casino

Only their hands are living, to the wheel attracted,
are moved, as deer trek desperately towards a creek
    through the dust and scrub of a desert, or gently,
        as sunflowers turn to the light,

and, as night takes up the cries of feverish children,
the cravings of lions in dens, the loves of dons,
    gathers them all and remains the night, the
        Great room is full of their prayers.

To a last feast of isolation self-invited,
they flock, and in a rite of disbelief are joined;
    from numbers all their stars are recreated,
        the enchanted, the worldly, the sad.

Without, calm rivers flow among the wholly living
quite near their trysts, and mountains part them, and birds,
    deep in the greens and moistures of summer,
        sing towards their work.

But here no nymph comes naked to the youngest shepherd,
the fountain is deserted, the laurel will not grow;
    the labyrinth is safe but endless, and broken
        is Ariadne's thread,

as deeper in these hands is grooved their fortune: lucky
were few, and it is possible that none was loved,
    and what was god-like in this generation
        was never to be born.

Oxford

Nature invades: old rooks in each college garden
Still talk, like agile babies, the language of feeling,
By towers a river still runs coastward and will run,
      Stones in those towers are utterly
      Satisfied still with their weight.

Mineral and creature, so deeply in love with themselves
Their sin of accidie excludes all others,
Challenge our high-strung students with a careless beauty,
      Setting a single error
      Against their countless faults.

Outside, some factories, then a whole green county
Where a cigarette comforts the evil, a hymn the weak,
Where thousands fidget and poke and spend their money:
      Eros Paidagogos
      Weeps on his virginal bed.

And over this talkative city like any other
Weep the non-attached angels. Here too the knowledge of death
Is a consuming love, and the natural heart refuses
      A low unflattering voice
      That sleeps not till it find a hearing.

Dover

Steep roads, a tunnel through chalk downs, are the approaches;
A ruined pharos overlooks a constructed bay;
The sea-front is almost elegant; all the show
Has, inland somewhere, a vague and dirty root:
      Nothing is made in this town.

A Norman castle, dominant, flood-lit at night,
Trains which fume in a station built on the sea,

Testify to the interests of its regular life:
Here dwell the experts on what the soldiers want,
    And who the travellers are

Whom ships carry in or out between the lighthouses,
Which guard for ever the made privacy of this bay
Like twin stone dogs opposed on a gentleman's gate.
Within these breakwaters English is properly spoken,
    Outside an atlas of tongues.

The eyes of departing migrants are fixed on the sea,
Conjuring destinies out of impersonal water:
'I see an important decision made on a lake,
An illness, a beard, Arabia found in a bed,
    Nanny defeated, Money.'

Red after years of failure or bright with fame,
The eyes of homecomers thank these historical cliffs:
'The mirror can no longer lie nor the clock reproach;
In the shadow under the yew, at the children's party,
    Everything must be explained.'

The Old Town with its Keep and Georgian houses
Has built its routine upon such unusual moments;
Vows, tears, emotional farewell gestures,
Are common here, unremarkable actions
    Like ploughing or a tipsy song.

Soldiers crowd into the pubs in their pretty clothes,
As pink and silly as girls from a high-class academy;
The Lion, The Rose, The Crown, will not ask them to die,
Not here, not now: all they are killing is time,
    A pauper civilian future.

Above them, expensive, shiny as a rich boy's bike,
Aeroplanes drone through the new European air
On the edge of a sky that makes England of minor importance;
And tides warn bronzing bathers of a cooling star
    With half its history done.

High over France, a full moon, cold and exciting
Like one of those dangerous flatterers we meet and love
When we are utterly wretched, returns our stare:
The night has found many recruits; to thousands of pilgrims
    The Mecca is coldness of heart.

The cries of the gulls at dawn are sad like work:
The soldier guards the traveller who pays for the soldier,
Each prays in a similar way for himself, but neither
Controls the years or the weather. Some may be heroes:
    Not all of us are unhappy.

Journey to Iceland

Each traveller prays *Let me be far from any*
physician, every port has its name for the sea,
    the citiless, the corroding, the sorrow,
      and North means to all *Reject.*

These plains are for ever where cold creatures are hunted
and on all sides: white wings flicker and flaunt;
    under a scolding flag the lover
      of islands may see at last,

in outline, his limited hope, as he nears a glitter
of glacier, sterile immature mountains intense
    in the abnormal northern day, and a river's
      fan-like polyp of sand.

Here let the citizen, then, find natural marvels,
a horse-shoe ravine, an issue of steam from a cleft
    in the rock, and rocks, and waterfalls brushing
      the rocks, and among the rocks birds;

the student of prose and conduct places to visit,
the site of a church where a bishop was put in a bag,
    the bath of a great historian, the fort where
      an outlaw dreaded the dark,

remember the doomed man thrown by his horse and crying
Beautiful is the hillside. I will not go,
the old woman confessing *He that I loved the*
best, to him I was worst.

Europe is absent: this is an island and should be
a refuge, where the affections of its dead can be bought
by those whose dreams accuse them of being
spitefully alive, and the pale

from too much passion of kissing feel pure in its deserts.
But is it, can they, as the world is and can lie?
A narrow bridge over a torrent,
a small farm under a crag

are natural settings for the jealousies of a province:
a weak vow of fidelity is made at a cairn,
within the indigenous figure on horseback
on the bridle-path down by the lake

his blood moves also by furtive and crooked inches,
asks all our questions: *Where is the homage? When*
shall justice be done? Who is against me?
Why am I always alone?'

Our time has no favourite suburb, no local features
are those of the young for whom all wish to care;
its promise is only a promise, the fabulous
country impartially far.

Tears fall in all the rivers: again some driver
pulls on his gloves and in a blinding snowstorm starts
upon a fatal journey, again some writer
runs howling to his art.

Detective Story

Who is ever quite without his landscape,
The straggling village street, the house in trees,
All near the church? Or else, the gloomy town-house,
The one with the Corinthian pillars, or
The tiny workmanlike flat, in any case
A home, a centre where the three or four things
That happen to a man do happen?
Who cannot draw the map of his life, shade in
The country station where he meets his loves
And says good-bye continually, mark the spot
Where the body of his happiness was first discovered?

An unknown tramp? A magnate? An enigma always,
With a well-buried past: and when the truth,
The truth about our happiness comes out,
How much it owed to blackmail and philandering.

What follows is habitual. All goes to plan:
The feud between the local common sense
And intuition, that exasperating amateur
Who's always on the spot by chance before us;
All goes to plan, both lying and confession,
Down to the thrilling final chase, the kill.

Yet, on the last page, a lingering doubt:
The verdict, was it just? The judge's nerves,
That clue, that protestation from the gallows,
And our own smile... why, yes...

But time is always guilty. Someone must pay for
Our loss of happiness, our happiness itself.

Death's Echo

'O who can ever gaze his fill,'
   Farmer and fisherman say,
'On native shore and local hill,
Grudge aching limb or callus on the hand?
Father, grandfather stood upon this land,
And here the pilgrims from our loins will stand.'
   So farmer and fisherman say
   In their fortunate hey-day:
   But Death's low answer drifts across
   Empty catch or harvest loss
     Or an unlucky May.
The earth is an oyster with nothing inside it,
   Not to be born is the best for man;
The end of toil is a bailiff's order,
   Throw down the mattock and dance while you can.

'O life's too short for friends who share,'
   Travellers think in their hearts,
'The city's common bed, the air,
The mountain bivouac and the bathing beach,
Where incidents draw every day from each
Memorable gesture and witty speech.'
   So travellers think in their hearts,
   Till malice or circumstance parts
Them from their constant humour:
And slyly Death's coercive rumour
   In that moment starts.
A friend is the old old tale of Narcissus,
   Not to be born is the best for man;
An active partner in something disgraceful,
   Change your partner, dance while you can.

'O stretch your hands across the sea,'
   The impassioned lover cries,
'Stretch them towards your harm and me.
Our grass is green, and sensual our brief bed,

The stream sings at its foot, and at its head
The mild and vegetarian beasts are fed.'
   So the impassioned lover cries
   Till the storm of pleasure dies:
From the bedpost and the rocks
Death's enticing echo mocks,
     And his voice replies.
The greater the love, the more false to its object,
   Not to be born is the best for man;
After the kiss comes the impulse to throttle,
   Break the embraces, dance while you can.

'I see the guilty world forgiven,'
   Dreamer and drunkard sing,
'The ladders let down out of heaven,
The laurel springing from the martyr's blood,
The children skipping where the weeper stood,
The lovers natural and the beasts all good.'
   So dreamer and drunkard sing
   Till day their sobriety bring:
Parrotwise with death's reply
From whelping fear and nesting lie,
     Woods and their echoes ring.
The desires of the heart are as crooked as corkscrews,
   Not to be born is the best for man;
The second-best is a formal order,
   The dance's pattern; dance while you can.
Dance, dance, for the figure is easy,
   The tune is catching and will not stop;
Dance till the stars come down from the rafters;
   Dance, dance, dance till you drop.

The Price

Who can ever praise enough
The world of his belief?
Harum-scarum childhood plays
In the meadows near his home,
In his woods love knows no wrong,
Travellers ride their placid ways,
In the cool shade of the tomb
Age's trusting footfalls ring.
Who can paint the vivid tree
And grass of phantasy?

But to create it and to guard
Shall be his whole reward:
He shall watch and he shall weep,
All his father's love deny,
To his mother's womb be lost,
Eight nights with a wanton sleep,
Then upon the ninth shall be
Bride and victim to a ghost,
And in the pit of terror thrown
Shall bear the wrath alone.

Danse Macabre

It's farewell to the drawing-room's mannerly cry,
The professor's logical whereto and why,
The frock-coated diplomat's polished aplomb,
Now matters are settled with gas and with bomb.

The works for two pianos, the brilliant stories
Of reasonable giants and remarkable fairies,
The pictures, the ointments, the frangible wares
And the branches of olive are stored upstairs.

For the Devil has broken parole and arisen,
He has dynamited his way out of prison,
Out of the well where his Papa throws
The rebel angel, the outcast rose.

Like influenza he walks abroad,
He stands by the bridge, he waits by the ford,
As a goose or a gull he flies overhead,
He hides in the cupboard and under the bed.

O were he to triumph, dear heart, you know
To what depths of shame he would drag you low;
He would steal you away from me, yes, my dear,
He would steal you and cut off your beautiful hair.

Millions already have come to their harm,
Succumbing like doves to his adder's charm;
Hundreds of trees in the wood are unsound:
I'm the axe that must cut them down to the ground.

For I, after all, am the Fortunate One,
The Happy-Go-Lucky, the spoilt Third Son;
For me it is written the Devil to chase
And to rid the earth of the human race.

The behaving of man is a world of horror,
A sedentary Sodom and slick Gomorrah;
I must take charge of the liquid fire
And storm the cities of human desire.

The buying and selling, the eating and drinking,
The disloyal machines and irreverent thinking,
The lovely dullards again and again
Inspiring their bitter ambitious men.

I shall come, I shall punish, the Devil be dead,
I shall have caviar thick on my bread,
I shall build myself a cathedral for home
With a vacuum cleaner in every room.

I shall ride the parade in a platinum car,
My features will shine, my name will be Star,
Day-long and night-long the bells I shall peal,
And down the long street I shall turn the cartwheel.

So Little John, Long John, Peter and Paul,
And poor little Horace with only one ball,
You shall leave your breakfast, your desk and your play
On a fine summer morning the Devil to slay.

For it's order and trumpet and anger and drum
And power and glory command you to come;
The graves will fly open to let you all in,
And the earth be emptied of mortal sin.

The fishes are silent deep in the sea,
The skies are lit up like a Christmas tree,
The star in the West shoots its warning cry:
'Mankind is alive, but Mankind must die.'

So good-bye to the house with its wallpaper red,
Good-bye to the sheets on the warm double bed,
Good-bye to the beautiful birds on the wall,
It's good-bye, dear heart, good-bye to you all.

Lullaby

Lay your sleeping head, my love,
Human on my faithless arm;
Time and fevers burn away
Individual beauty from
Thoughtful children, and the grave
Proves the child ephemeral:
But in my arms till break of day
Let the living creature lie,
Mortal, guilty, but to me
The entirely beautiful.

Soul and body have no bounds:
To lovers as they lie upon
Her tolerant enchanted slope
In their ordinary swoon,
Grave the vision Venus sends
Of supernatural sympathy,
Universal love and hope;
While an abstract insight wakes
Among the glaciers and the rocks
The hermit's carnal ecstasy.

Certainty, fidelity
On the stroke of midnight pass
Like vibrations of a bell
And fashionable madmen raise
Their pedantic boring cry:
Every farthing of the cost,
All the dreaded cards foretell,
Shall be paid, but from this night
Not a whisper, not a thought,
Not a kiss nor look be lost.

Beauty, midnight, vision dies:
Let the winds of dawn that blow
Softly round your dreaming head
Such a day of welcome show
Eye and knocking heart may bless,
Find our mortal world enough;
Noons of dryness find you fed
By the involuntary powers,
Nights of insult let you pass
Watched by every human love.

Orpheus

What does the song hope for? And his moved hands
A little way from the birds, the shy, the delightful?
      To be bewildered and happy,
      Or most of all the knowledge of life?

But the beautiful are content with the sharp notes of the air;
The warmth is enough. O if winter really
      Oppose, if the weak snowflake,
      What will the wish, what will the dance do?

Miss Gee

Let me tell you a little story
    About Miss Edith Gee;
She lived in Clevedon Terrace
    At Number 83.

She'd a slight squint in her left eye,
    Her lips they were thin and small,
She had narrow sloping shoulders
    And she had no bust at all.

She'd a velvet hat with trimmings,
    And a dark grey serge costume;
She lived in Clevedon Terrace
    In a small bed-sitting room.

She'd a purple mac for wet days,
    A green umbrella too to take,
She'd a bicycle with shopping basket
    And a harsh back-pedal brake.

The Church of Saint Aloysius
    Was not so very far;
She did a lot of knitting,
    Knitting for that Church Bazaar.

Miss Gee looked up at the starlight
    And said, 'Does anyone care
That I live in Clevedon Terrace
    On one hundred pounds a year?'

She dreamed a dream one evening
    That she was the Queen of France
And the Vicar of Saint Aloysius
    Asked Her Majesty to dance.

But a storm blew down the palace,
    She was biking through a field of corn,
And a bull with the face of the Vicar
    Was charging with lowered horn.

She could feel his hot breath behind her,
    He was going to overtake;
And the bicycle went slower and slower
    Because of that back-pedal brake.

Summer made the trees a picture,
    Winter made them a wreck;
She bicycled to the evening service
    With her clothes buttoned up to her neck.

She passed by the loving couples,
    She turned her head away;
She passed by the loving couples
    And they didn't ask her to stay.

Miss Gee sat down in the side-aisle,
    She heard the organ play;
And the choir it sang so sweetly
    At the ending of the day,

Miss Gee knelt down in the side-aisle,
    She knelt down on her knees;
'Lead me not into temptation
    But make me a good girl, please.'

The days and nights went by her
    Like waves round a Cornish wreck;
She bicycled down to the doctor
    With her clothes buttoned up to her neck.

She bicycled down to the doctor,
    And rang the surgery bell;
'O, doctor, I've a pain inside me,
    And I don't feel very well.'

Doctor Thomas looked her over,
    And then he looked some more;
Walked over to his wash-basin,
    Said, 'Why didn't you come before?'

Doctor Thomas sat over his dinner,
    Though his wife was waiting to ring,
Rolling his bread into pellets;
    Said, 'Cancer's a funny thing.

'Nobody knows what the cause is,
    Though some pretend they do;
It's like some hidden assassin
    Waiting to strike at you.

'Childless women get it,
    And men when they retire;
It's as if there had to be some outlet
    For their foiled creative fire.'

His wife she rang for the servant,
    Said, 'Don't be so morbid, dear';
He said: 'I saw Miss Gee this evening
    And she's a goner, I fear.'

They took Miss Gee to the hospital,
    She lay there a total wreck,
Lay in the ward for women
    With the bedclothes right up to her neck.

They laid her on the table,
    The students began to laugh;
And Mr. Rose the surgeon
    He cut Miss Gee in half.

Mr. Rose he turned to his students,
    Said, 'Gentlemen, if you please,
We seldom see a sarcoma
    As far advanced as this.'

They took her off the table,
    They wheeled away Miss Gee
Down to another department
    Where they study Anatomy.

They hung her from the ceiling,
    Yes, they hung up Miss Gee;
And a couple of Oxford Groupers
    Carefully dissected her knee.

Victor

Victor was a little baby,
        Into this world he came;
His father took him on his knee and said:
        'Don't dishonour the family name.'

Victor looked up at his father
        Looked up with big round eyes:
His father said; 'Victor, my only son,
        Don't you ever ever tell lies.'

Victor and his father went riding
        Out in a little dog-cart;
His father took a Bible from his pocket and read,
        'Blessed are the pure in heart.'

It was a frosty December,
          It wasn't the season for fruits;
His father fell dead of heart disease
          While lacing up his boots.

It was a frosty December
          When into his grave he sank;
His uncle found Victor a post as cashier
          In the Midland Counties Bank.

It was a frosty December
          Victor was only eighteen,
But his figures were neat and his margins straight
          And his cuffs were always clean.

He took a room at the Peveril,
          A respectable boarding-house;
And Time watched Victor day after day
          As a cat will watch a mouse.

The clerks slapped Victor on the shoulder;
          'Have you ever had a woman?' they said,
'Come down town with us on Saturday night'.
          Victor smiled and shook his head.

The manager sat in his office,
          Smoked a Corona cigar:
Said; 'Victor's a decent fellow but
          He's too mousey to go far'.

Victor went up to his bedroom,
          Set the alarum bell;
Climbed into bed, took his Bible and read
          Of what happened to Jezebel.

It was the First of April,
          Anna to the Peveril came;
Her eyes, her lips, her breasts, her hips
          And her smile set men aflame.

She looked as pure as a schoolgirl
    On her First Communion day,
But her kisses were like the best champagne
    When she gave herself away.

It was the Second of April,
    She was wearing a coat of fur;
Victor met her upon the stairs
    And he fell in love with her.

The first time he made his proposal,
    She laughed, said; 'I'll never wed':
The second time there was a pause;
    Then she smiled and shook her head.

Anna looked into her mirror,
    Pouted and gave a frown:
Said; 'Victor's as dull as a wet afternoon
    But I've got to settle down.'

The third time he made his proposal,
    As they walked by the Reservoir:
She gave him a kiss like a blow on the head,
    Said; 'You are my heart's desire.'

They were married early in August,
    She said; 'Kiss me, you funny boy':
Victor took her in his arms and said;
    'O my Helen of Troy.'

It was the middle of September,
    Victor came to the office one day;
He was wearing a flower in his buttonhole,
    He was late but he was gay.

The clerks were talking of Anna,
    The door was just ajar:
One said; 'Poor old Victor, but where ignorance
    Is bliss, et cetera.'

Victor stood still as a statue,
        The door was just ajar:
One said; 'God, what fun I had with her
        In that Baby Austin car.'

Victor walked out into the High Street,
        He walked to the edge of the town;
He came to the allotments and the rubbish heap;
        And his tears came tumbling down.

Victor looked up at the sunset
        As he stood there all alone;
Cried; 'Are you in Heaven, Father?'
        But the sky said 'Address not known'.

Victor looked up at the mountains,
        The mountains all covered with snow;
Cried; 'Are you pleased with me, Father?'
        And the answer came back, 'No'.

Victor came to the forest,
        Cried; 'Father, will she ever be true?'
And the oaks and the beeches shook their heads
        And they answered; 'Not to you.'

Victor came to the meadow
        Where the wind went sweeping by:
Cried; 'O Father, I love her so',
        But the wind said; 'She must die'.

Victor came to the river
        Running so deep and so still:
Cried; 'O Father, what shall I do?'
        And the river answered; 'Kill'.

Anna was sitting at a table,
        Drawing cards from a pack;
Anna was sitting at table
        Waiting for her husband to come back.

It wasn't the Jack of Diamonds
        Nor the Joker she drew at first;
It wasn't the King or the Queen of Hearts
        But the Ace of Spades reversed.

Victor stood in the doorway,
        He didn't utter a word:
She said; 'What's the matter, darling?'
        He behaved as if he hadn't heard.

There was a voice in his left ear,
        There was a voice in his right,
There was a voice at the base of his skull
        Saying: 'She must die to-night'.

Victor picked up a carving-knife,
        His features were set and drawn,
Said; 'Anna, it would have been better for you
        If you had not been born.'

Anna jumped up from the table,
        Anna started to scream,
But Victor came slowly after her
        Like a horror in a dream.

She dodged behind the sofa,
        She tore down a curtain rod,
But Victor came slowly after her:
        Said; 'Prepare to meet thy God.'

She managed to wrench the door open,
        She ran and she didn't stop.
But Victor followed her up the stairs
        And he caught her at the top.

He stood there above the body,
        He stood there holding the knife;
And the blood ran down the stairs and sang;
        'I'm the Resurrection and the Life'.

They tapped Victor on the shoulder,
    They took him away in a van;
He sat as quiet as a lump of moss
    Saying, 'I am the Son of Man'.

Victor sat in a corner
    Making a woman of clay:
Saying; 'I am Alpha and Omega, I shall come
    To judge the earth one day.'

As He Is

Wrapped in a yielding air, beside
    The flower's noiseless hunger,
Close to the tree's clandestine tide,
    Close to the bird's high fever,
    Loud in his hope and anger,
Erect about a skeleton,
    Stands the expressive lover,
    Stands the deliberate man.

Beneath the hot unasking sun,
    Past stronger beasts and fairer
He picks his way, a living gun,
    With gun and lens and Bible,
    A militant enquirer,
The friend, the rash, the enemy,
    The essayist, the able,
    Able at times to cry.

The friendless and unhated stone
    Lies everywhere about him,
The Brothered-One, the Not-Alone,
    The brothered and the hated
    Whose family have taught him
To set against the large and dumb,
    The timeless and the rooted,
    His money and his time.

For mother's fading hopes become
 Dull wives to his dull spirits,
Soon dulled by nurse's moral thumb,
 That dullard fond betrayer,
 And, childish, he inherits,
So soon by legal father tricked,
 The tall imposing tower,
 Imposing, yes, but locked.

And ruled by dead men never met,
 By pious guess deluded,
Upon the stool of mania set
 Or stool of desolation,
 Sits murderous and clear-headed;
Enormous beauties round him move,
 For grandiose is his vision
 And grandiose his love.

Determined on Time's truthful shield
 The lamb must face the tigress,
Their faithful quarrel never healed
 Though, faithless, he consider
 His dream of vaguer ages,
Hunter and victim reconciled,
 The lion and the adder,
 The adder and the child.

Fresh loves betray him, every day
 Over his green horizon
A fresh deserter rides away,
 And miles away birds mutter
 Of ambush and of treason;
To fresh defeats he still must move,
 To further griefs and greater,
 And the defeat of grief.

A Voyage

I. WHITHER?

Where does this journey look which the watcher upon the quay,
Standing under his evil star, so bitterly envies,
As the mountains swim away with slow calm strokes
And the gulls abandon their vow? Does it promise a juster life?

Alone with his heart at last, does the fortunate traveller find
In the vague touch of a breeze, the fickle flash of a wave,
Proofs that somewhere exists, really, the Good Place,
Convincing as those that children find in stones and holes?

No, he discovers nothing: he does not want to arrive.
His journey is false, his unreal excitement really an illness
On a false island where the heart cannot act and will not suffer:
He condones his fever; he is weaker than he thought; his weakness
    is real.

But at moments, as when real dolphins with leap and panache
Cajole for recognition or, far away, a real island
Gets up to catch his eye, his trance is broken: he remembers
Times and places where he was well; he believes in joy,

That, maybe, his fever shall find a cure, the true journey an end
Where hearts meet and are really true, and crossed this ocean, that
    parts
Hearts which alter but is the same always, that goes
Everywhere, as truth and falsehood go, but cannot suffer.

II. THE SHIP

All streets are brightly lit; our city is kept clean;
Her Third-Class deal from greasy packs, her First bid high;
Her beggars banished to the bows have never seen
What can be done in state-rooms: no one asks why.

Lovers are writing letters, athletes playing ball,
One doubts the virtue, one the beauty of his wife,
A boy's ambitious: perhaps the Captain hates us all;
Someone perhaps is leading a civilised life.

Slowly our Western culture in full pomp progresses
Over the barren plains of a sea; somewhere ahead
A septic East, odd fowl and flowers, odder dresses:

Somewhere a strange and shrewd To-morrow goes to bed,
Planning a test for men from Europe; no one guesses
Who will be most ashamed, who richer, and who dead.

III. THE SPHINX

Did it once issue from the carver's hand
Healthy? Even the earliest conqueror saw
The face of a sick ape, a bandaged paw,
An ailing lion crouched on dirty sand.

We gape, then go uneasily away:
It does not like the young nor love nor learning.
Time hurt it like a person: it lies turning
A vast behind on shrill America,

And witnesses. The huge hurt face accuses
And pardons nothing, least of all success:
What counsel it might offer it refuses
To those who face akimbo its distress.

'Do people like me?' *No*. The slave amuses
The lion. 'Am I to suffer always?' *Yes*.

IV. HONG KONG

Its leading characters are wise and witty,
Their suits well-tailored, and they wear them well,
Have many a polished parable to tell
About the *mores* of a trading city.

Only the servants enter unexpected,
Their silent movements make dramatic news;
Here in the East our bankers have erected
A worthy temple to the Comic Muse.

Ten thousand miles from home and What's-Her-Name
A bugle on this Late Victorian hill
Puts out the soldier's light; off-stage, a war

Thuds like the slamming of a distant door:
Each has his comic role in life to fill,
Though Life be neither comic nor a game.

V. MACAO

A weed from Catholic Europe, it took root
Between some yellow mountains and a sea,
Its gay stone houses an exotic fruit,
A Portugal-cum-China oddity.

Rococo images of Saint and Saviour
Promise its gamblers fortunes when they die,
Churches alongside brothels testify
That faith can pardon natural behavior.

A town of such indulgence need not fear
Those mortal sins by which the strong are killed
And limbs and governments are torn to pieces:

Religious clocks will strike, the childish vices
Will safeguard the low virtues of the child,
And nothing serious can happen here.

VI. A MAJOR PORT

No guidance can be found in ancient lore:
Banks jostle in the sun for domination,
Behind them stretch like sorry vegetation
The low recessive houses of the poor.

We have no destiny assigned us,
No data but our bodies: we plan
To better ourselves; bleak hospitals alone remind us
Of the equality of man.

Children are really loved here, even by police:
They speak of years before the big were lonely.
Here will be no recurrence.

                    Only
The brass-bands throbbing in the parks foretell
Some future reign of happiness and peace.

We learn to pity and rebel.

The Capital

Quarter of pleasures where the rich are always waiting,
Waiting expensively for miracles to happen,
Dim-lighted restaurant where lovers eat each other,
Café where exiles have established a malicious village:

You with your charm and your apparatus have abolished
The strictness of winter and the spring's compulsion;
Far from your lights the outraged punitive father,
The dullness of mere obedience here is apparent.

So with orchestras and glances, soon you betray us
To belief in our infinite powers; and the innocent
Unobservant offender falls in a moment
Victim to his heart's invisible furies.

In unlighted streets you hide away the appalling;
Factories where lives are made for a temporary use
Like collars or chairs, rooms where the lonely are battered
Slowly like pebbles into fortuitous shapes.

But the sky you illumine, your glow is visible far
Into the dark countryside, enormous and frozen,
Where, hinting at the forbidden like a wicked uncle,
Night after night to the farmer's children you beckon.

Brussels in Winter

Wandering through cold streets tangled like old string,
Coming on fountains rigid in the frost,
Its formula escapes you; it has lost
The certainty that constitutes a thing.

Only the old, the hungry and the humbled
Keep at this temperature a sense of place,
And in their misery are all assembled;
The winter holds them like an Opera-House.

Ridges of rich apartments loom to-night
Where isolated windows glow like farms,
A phrase goes packed with meaning like a van,

A look contains the history of man,
And fifty francs will earn a stranger right
To take the shuddering city in his arms.

Musée des Beaux Arts

About suffering they were never wrong,
The Old Masters: how well they understood
Its human position; how it takes place
While someone else is eating or opening a window or just walking
    dully along;
How, when the aged are reverently, passionately waiting
For the miraculous birth, there always must be
Children who did not specially want it to happen, skating
On a pond at the edge of the wood:

They never forgot
That even the dreadful martyrdom must run its course
Anyhow in a corner, some untidy spot
Where the dogs go on with their doggy life and the torturer's
    horse
Scratches its innocent behind on a tree.

In Brueghel's *Icarus*, for instance: how everything turns away
Quite leisurely from the disaster; the ploughman may
Have heard the splash, the forsaken cry,
But for him it was not an important failure; the sun shone
As it had to on the white legs disappearing into the green
Water; and the expensive delicate ship that must have seen
Something amazing, a boy falling out of the sky,
Had somewhere to get to and sailed calmly on.

Gare du Midi

A nondescript express in from the South,
Crowds round the ticket barrier, a face
To welcome which the mayor has not contrived
Bugles or braid: something about the mouth
Distracts the stray look with alarm and pity.
Snow is falling. Clutching a little case,
He walks out briskly to infect a city
Whose terrible future may have just arrived.

The Novelist

Encased in talent like a uniform,
The rank of every poet is well known;
They can amaze us like a thunderstorm,
Or die so young, or live for years alone.

They can dash forward like hussars: but he
Must struggle out of his boyish gift and learn
How to be plain and awkward, how to be
One after whom none think it worth to turn.

For, to achieve his lightest wish, he must
Become the whole of boredom, subject to
Vulgar complaints like love, among the Just

Be just, among the Filthy filthy too,
And in his own weak person, if he can,
Dully put up with all the wrongs of Man.

The Composer

All the others translate: the painter sketches
A visible world to love or reject;
Rummaging into his living, the poet fetches
The images out that hurt and connect,

From Life to Art by painstaking adaption,
Relying on us to cover the rift;
Only your notes are pure contraption,
Only your song is an absolute gift.

Pour out your presence, a delight cascading
The falls of the knee and the weirs of the spine,
Our climate of silence and doubt invading;

You alone, alone, imaginary song,
Are unable to say an existence is wrong,
And pour out your forgiveness like a wine.

Rimbaud

The nights, the railway-arches, the bad sky,
His horrible companions did not know it;
But in that child the rhetorician's lie
Burst like a pipe: the cold had made a poet.

Drinks bought him by his weak and lyric friend
His five wits systematically deranged,
To all accustomed nonsense put an end;
Till he from lyre and weakness was estranged.

Verse was a special illness of the ear;
Integrity was not enough; that seemed
The hell of childhood: he must try again.

Now, galloping through Africa, he dreamed
Of a new self, a son, an engineer,
His truth acceptable to lying men.

A. E. Housman

No one, not even Cambridge, was to blame
(Blame if you like the human situation):
Heart-injured in North London, he became
The Latin Scholar of his generation.

Deliberately he chose the dry-as-dust,
Kept tears like dirty postcards in a drawer;
Food was his public love, his private lust
Something to do with violence and the poor.

In savage foot-notes on unjust editions
He timidly attacked the life he led,
And put the money of his feelings on

The uncritical relations of the dead,
Where only geographical divisions
Parted the coarse hanged soldier from the don.

Edward Lear

Left by his friend to breakfast alone on the white
Italian shore, his Terrible Demon arose
Over his shoulder; he wept to himself in the night,
A dirty landscape-painter who hated his nose.

The legions of cruel inquisitive They
Were so many and big like dogs: he was upset
By Germans and boats; affection was miles away:
But guided by tears he successfully reached his Regret.

How prodigious the welcome was. Flowers took his hat
And bore him off to introduce him to the tongs;
The demon's false nose made the table laugh; a cat
Soon had him waltzing madly, let him squeeze her hand;
Words pushed him to the piano to sing comic songs;

And children swarmed to him like settlers. He became a land.

Epitaph on a Tyrant

Perfection, of a kind, was what he was after,
And the poetry he invented was easy to understand;
He knew human folly like the back of his hand,
And was greatly interested in armies and fleets;
When he laughed, respectable senators burst with laughter,
And when he cried the little children died in the streets.

Sonnets from China

I

So from the years their gifts were showered: each
Grabbed at the one it needed to survive;
Bee took the politics that suit a hive,
Trout finned as trout, peach moulded into peach,

And were successful at their first endeavour.
The hour of birth their only time in college,
They were content with their precocious knowledge,
To know their station and be right for ever.

Till, finally, there came a childish creature
On whom the years could model any feature,
Fake, as chance fell, a leopard or a dove,

Who by the gentlest wind was rudely shaken,
Who looked for truth but always was mistaken,
And envied his few friends, and chose his love.

II

They wondered why the fruit had been forbidden:
It taught them nothing new. They hid their pride,
But did not listen much when they were chidden:
They knew exactly what to do outside.

They left. Immediately the memory faded
Of all they'd known: they could not understand
The dogs now who before had always aided;
The stream was dumb with whom they'd always planned.

They wept and quarrelled: freedom was so wild.
In front maturity as he ascended
Retired like a horizon from the child,

The dangers and the punishments grew greater,
And the way back by angels was defended
Against the poet and the legislator.

III

Only a smell had feelings to make known,
Only an eye could point in a direction,
The fountain's utterance was itself alone:
He, though, by naming thought to make connection

Between himself as hunter and his food;
He felt the interest in his throat and found
That he could send a servant to chop wood
Or kiss a girl to rapture with a sound.

They bred like locusts till they hid the green
And edges of the world: confused and abject,
A creature to his own creation subject,

He shook with hate for things he'd never seen,
Pined for a love abstracted from its object,
And was oppressed as he had never been.

IV

He stayed, and was imprisoned in possession:
By turns the seasons guarded his one way,
The mountains chose the mother of his children,
In lieu of conscience the sun ruled his day.

Beyond him, his young cousins in the city
Pursued their rapid and unnatural courses,
Believed in nothing but were easy-going,
Far less afraid of strangers than of horses.

He, though, changed little,
But took his colour from the earth,
And grew in likeness to his fowls and cattle.

The townsman thought him miserly and simple,
Unhappy poets took him for the truth,
And tyrants held him up as an example.

V

His care-free swagger was a fine invention:
Life was too slow, too regular, too grave.
With horse and sword he drew the girls' attention,
A conquering hero, bountiful and brave,

To whom teen-agers looked for liberation:
At his command they left behind their mothers,
Their wits were sharpened by the long migration,
His camp-fires taught them all the horde were brothers.

Till what he came to do was done: unwanted,
Grown seedy, paunchy, pouchy, disappointed,
He took to drink to screw his nerves to murder,

Or sat in offices and stole,
Boomed at his children about Law and Order,
And hated life with heart and soul.

VI

He watched the stars and noted birds in flight;
A river flooded or a fortress fell:
He made predictions that were sometimes right;
His lucky guesses were rewarded well.

Falling in love with Truth before he knew Her,
He rode into imaginary lands,
By solitude and fasting hoped to woo Her,
And mocked at those who served Her with their hands.

Drawn as he was to magic and obliqueness,
In Her he honestly believed, and when
At last She beckoned to him he obeyed,

Looked in Her eyes: awe-struck but unafraid,
Saw there reflected every human weakness,
And knew himself as one of many men.

VII

He was their servant (some say he was blind),
Who moved among their faces and their things:
Their feeling gathered in him like a wind
And sang. They cried 'It is a God that sings',

And honoured him, a person set apart,
Till he grew vain, mistook for personal song
The petty tremors of his mind or heart
At each domestic wrong.

Lines came to him no more; he had to make them
(With what precision was each strophe planned):
Hugging his gloom as peasants hug their land,

He stalked like an assassin through the town,
And glared at men because he did not like them,
But trembled if one passed him with a frown.

VIII

He turned his field into a meeting-place,
Evolved a tolerant ironic eye,
Put on a mobile money-changer's face,
Took up the doctrine of Equality.

Strangers were hailed as brothers by his clocks,
With roof and spire he built a human sky,
Stored random facts in a museum box,
To watch his treasure set a paper spy.

All grew so fast his life was overgrown,
Till he forgot what all had once been made for:
He gathered into crowds but was alone,

And lived expensively but did without,
No more could touch the earth which he had paid for,
Nor feel the love which he knew all about.

IX

He looked in all His wisdom from His throne
Down on the humble boy who herded sheep,
And sent a dove. The dove returned alone:
Song put a charmed rusticity to sleep.

But He had planned such future for this youth:
Surely, His duty now was to compel,
To count on time to bring true love of truth
And, with it, gratitude. His eagle fell.

It did not work: His conversation bored
The boy, who yawned and whistled and made faces,
And wriggled free from fatherly embraces,

But with His messenger was always willing
To go where it suggested, and adored,
And learned from it so many ways of killing.

X

So an age ended, and its last deliverer died
In bed, grown idle and unhappy; they were safe:
The sudden shadow of a giant's enormous calf
Would fall no more at dusk across their lawns outside.

They slept in peace: in marshes here and there no doubt
A sterile dragon lingered to a natural death,
But in a year the slot had vanished from the heath;
A kobold's knocking in the mountain petered out.

Only the sculptors and the poets were half-sad,
And the pert retinue from the magician's house
Grumbled and went elsewhere. The vanquished powers
     were glad

To be invisible and free; without remorse
Struck down the silly sons who strayed into their course,
And ravished the daughters, and drove the fathers mad.

XI

Certainly praise: let song mount again and again
For life as it blossoms out in a jar or a face,
For vegetal patience, for animal courage and grace:
Some have been happy; some, even, were great men.

But hear the morning's injured weeping and know why:
Ramparts and souls have fallen; the will of the unjust
Has never lacked an engine; still all princes must
Employ the fairly-noble unifying lie.

History opposes its grief to our buoyant song,
To our hope its warning. One star has warmed to birth
One puzzled species that has yet to prove its worth:

The quick new West is false, and prodigious but wrong
The flower-like Hundred Families who for so long
In the Eighteen Provinces have modified the earth.

XII

Here war is harmless like a monument:
A telephone is talking to a man;
Flags on a map declare that troops were sent;
A boy brings milk in bowls. There is a plan

For living men in terror of their lives,
Who thirst at nine who were to thirst at noon,
Who can be lost and are, who miss their wives
And, unlike an idea, can die too soon.

Yet ideas can be true, although men die:
For we have seen a myriad faces
Ecstatic from one lie,

And maps can really point to places
Where life is evil now.
Nanking. Dachau.

133

XIII

Far from a cultural centre he was used:
Abandoned by his general and his lice,
Under a padded quilt he turned to ice
And vanished. He will never be perused

When this campaign is tidied into books:
No vital knowledge perished in that skull;
His jokes were stale; like wartime, he was dull;
His name is lost for ever like his looks.

Though runeless, to instructions from headquarters
He added meaning like a comma when
He joined the dust of China, that our daughters

Might keep their upright carriage, not again
Be shamed before the dogs, that, where are waters,
Mountains and houses, may be also men.

XIV

They are and suffer; that is all they do:
A bandage hides the place where each is living,
His knowledge of the world restricted to
A treatment metal instruments are giving.

They lie apart like epochs from each other
(Truth in their sense is how much they can bear;
It is not talk like ours but groans they smother),
From us remote as plants: we stand elsewhere.

For who when healthy can become a foot?
Even a scratch we can't recall when cured,
But are boisterous in a moment and believe

Reality is never injured, cannot
Imagine isolation: joy can be shared,
And anger, and the idea of love.

XV

As evening fell the day's oppression lifted;
Tall peaks came into focus; it had rained:
Across wide lawns and cultured flowers drifted
The conversation of the highly trained.

Thin gardeners watched them pass and priced their shoes;
A chauffeur waited, reading in the drive,
For them to finish their exchange of views:
It looked a picture of the way to live.

Far off, no matter what good they intended,
Two armies waited for a verbal error
With well-made implements for causing pain,

And on the issue of their charm depended
A land laid waste with all its young men slain,
Its women weeping, and its towns in terror.

XVI

Our global story is not yet completed,
Crime, daring, commerce, chatter will go on,
But, as narrators find their memory gone,
Homeless, disterred, these know themselves defeated.

Some could not like nor change the young and mourn for
Some wounded myth that once made children good,
Some lost a world they never understood,
Some saw too clearly all that man was born for.

Loss is their shadow-wife, Anxiety
Receives them like a grand hotel, but where
They may regret they must: their doom to bear

Love for some far forbidden country, see
A native disapprove them with a stare
And Freedom's back in every door and tree.

XVII

Simple like all dream-wishes, they employ
The elementary rhythms of the heart,
Speak to our muscles of a need for joy:
The dying and the lovers bound to part

Hear them and have to whistle. Ever new,
They mirror every change in our position,
They are our evidence of how we do,
The very echoes of our lost condition.

Think in this year what pleased the dancers best,
When Austria died, when China was forsaken,
Shanghai in flames and Teruel re-taken.

France put her case before the world: *Partout
Il y a de la joie*. America addressed
Mankind: *Do you love me as I love you?*

XVIII

Chilled by the Present, its gloom and its noise,
On waking we sigh for an ancient South,
A warm nude age of instinctive poise,
A taste of joy in an innocent mouth.

At night in our huts we dream of a part
In the balls of the Future: each ritual maze
Has a musical plan, and a musical heart
Can faultlessly follow its faultless ways.

We envy streams and houses that are sure,
But, doubtful, articled to error, we
Were never nude and calm as a great door,

And never will be faultless like our fountains:
We live in freedom by necessity,
A mountain people dwelling among mountains.

XIX

When all our apparatus of report
Confirms the triumph of our enemies,
Our frontier crossed, our forces in retreat,
Violence pandemic like a new disease,

And Wrong a charmer everywhere invited,
When Generosity gets nothing done,
Let us remember those who looked deserted:
To-night in China let me think of one

Who for ten years of drought and silence waited,
Until in Muzot all his being spoke,
And everything was given once for all.

Awed, grateful, tired, content to die, completed,
He went out in the winter night to stroke
That tower as one pets an animal.

XX

Who needs their names? Another genus built
Those dictatorial avenues and squares,
Gigantic terraces, imposing stairs,
Men of a sorry kennel, racked by guilt,

Who wanted to persist in stone for ever:
Unloved, they had to leave material traces,
But these desired no statues but our faces,
To dwell there incognito, glad we never

Can dwell on what they suffered, loved or were.
Earth grew them as a bay grows fishermen
Or hills a shepherd. While they breathed, the air

All breathe took on a virtue; in our blood,
If we allow them, they can breathe again:
Happy their wish and mild to flower and flood.

XXI

(To E. M. Forster)

Though Italy and King's are far away,
And Truth a subject only bombs discuss,
Our ears unfriendly, still you speak to us,
Insisting that the inner life can pay.

As we dash down the slope of hate with gladness,
You trip us up like an unnoticed stone,
And, just when we are closeted with madness,
You interrupt us like the telephone.

Yes, we are Lucy, Turton, Philip: we
Wish international evil, are delighted
To join the jolly ranks of the benighted

Where reason is denied and love ignored,
But, as we swear our lie, Miss Avery
Comes out into the garden with a sword.

Part III
1939-1947

In Memory of W. B. Yeats

(*d. Jan.* 1939)

I

He disappeared in the dead of winter:
The brooks were frozen, the airports almost deserted,
And snow disfigured the public statues;
The mercury sank in the mouth of the dying day.
What instruments we have agree
The day of his death was a dark cold day.

Far from his illness
The wolves ran on through the evergreen forests,
The peasant river was untempted by the fashionable quays;
By mourning tongues
The death of the poet was kept from his poems.

But for him it was his last afternoon as himself,
An afternoon of nurses and rumours;
The provinces of his body revolted,
The squares of his mind were empty,
Silence invaded the suburbs,
The current of his feeling failed; he became his admirers.

Now he is scattered among a hundred cities
And wholly given over to unfamiliar affections,
To find his happiness in another kind of wood
And be punished under a foreign code of conscience.
The words of a dead man
Are modified in the guts of the living.

But in the importance and noise of to-morrow
When the brokers are roaring like beasts on the floor of the Bourse,
And the poor have the sufferings to which they are fairly
    accustomed,
And each in the cell of himself is almost convinced of his freedom,
A few thousand will think of this day
As one thinks of a day when one did something slightly unusual.
What instruments we have agree
The day of his death was a dark cold day.

II

You were silly like us; your gift survived it all:
The parish of rich women, physical decay,
Yourself. Mad Ireland hurt you into poetry.
Now Ireland has her madness and her weather still,
For poetry makes nothing happen: it survives
In the valley of its making where executives
Would never want to tamper, flows on south
From ranches of isolation and the busy griefs,
Raw towns that we believe and die in; it survives,
A way of happening, a mouth.

III

Earth, receive an honoured guest:
William Yeats is laid to rest.
Let the Irish vessel lie
Emptied of its poetry.

In the nightmare of the dark
All the dogs of Europe bark,
And the living nations wait,
Each sequestered in its hate;

Intellectual disgrace
Stares from every human face,
And the seas of pity lie
Locked and frozen in each eye.

Follow, poet, follow right
To the bottom of the night,
With your unconstraining voice
Still persuade us to rejoice;

With the farming of a verse
Make a vineyard of the curse,
Sing of human unsuccess
In a rapture of distress;

In the deserts of the heart
Let the healing fountain start,
In the prison of his days
Teach the free man how to praise.

In Memory of Ernst Toller

(d. May 1939)

The shining neutral summer has no voice
To judge America, or ask how a man dies;
And the friends who are sad and the enemies who rejoice

Are chased by their shadows lightly away from the grave
Of one who was egotistical and brave,
Lest they should learn without suffering how to forgive.

What was it, Ernst, that your shadow unwittingly said?
Did the small child see something horrid in the woodshed
Long ago? Or had the Europe which took refuge in your head

Already been too injured to get well?
For just how long, like the swallows in that other cell,
Had the bright little longings been flying in to tell

About the big and friendly death outside,
Where people do not occupy or hide;
No towns like Munich; no need to write?

Dear Ernst, lie shadowless at last among
The other war-horses who existed till they'd done
Something that was an example to the young.

We are lived by powers we pretend to understand:
They arrange our loves; it is they who direct at the end
The enemy bullet, the sickness, or even our hand.

It is their to-morrow hangs over the earth of the living
And all that we wish for our friends: but existence is believing
We know for whom we mourn and who is grieving.

Voltaire at Ferney

Almost happy now, he looked at his estate.
An exile making watches glanced up as he passed,
And went on working; where a hospital was rising fast
A joiner touched his cap; an agent came to tell
Some of the trees he'd planted were progressing well.
The white alps glittered. It was summer. He was very great.

Far off in Paris, where his enemies
Whispered that he was wicked, in an upright chair
A blind old woman longed for death and letters. He would write
'Nothing is better than life'. But was it? Yes, the fight
Against the false and the unfair
Was always worth it. So was gardening. Civilize.

Cajoling, scolding, scheming, cleverest of them all,
He'd led the other children in a holy war
Against the infamous grown-ups, and, like a child, been sly
And humble when there was occasion for
The two-faced answer or the plain protective lie,
But, patient like a peasant, waited for their fall.

And never doubted, like D'Alembert, he would win:
Only Pascal was a great enemy, the rest

Were rats already poisoned; there was much, though, to be done,
And only himself to count upon.
Dear Diderot was dull but did his best;
Rousseau, he'd always known, would blubber and give in.

So, like a sentinel, he could not sleep. The night was full of wrong,
Earthquakes and executions. Soon he would be dead,
And still all over Europe stood the horrible nurses
Itching to boil their children. Only his verses
Perhaps could stop them: He must go on working. Overhead
The uncomplaining stars composed their lucid song.

Herman Melville

(For Lincoln Kirstein)

Towards the end he sailed into an extraordinary mildness,
And anchored in his home and reached his wife
And rode within the harbour of her hand,
And went across each morning to an office
As though his occupation were another island.

Goodness existed: that was the new knowledge.
His terror had to blow itself quite out
To let him see it; but it was the gale had blown him
Past the Cape Horn of sensible success
Which cries: 'This rock is Eden. Shipwreck here.'

But deafened him with thunder and confused with lightning:
— The maniac hero hunting like a jewel
The rare ambiguous monster that had maimed his sex,
Hatred for hatred ending in a scream,
The unexplained survivor breaking off the nightmare —
All that was intricate and false; the truth was simple.

Evil is unspectacular and always human,
And shares our bed and eats at our own table,
And we are introduced to Goodness every day,

Even in drawing-rooms among a crowd of faults;
He has a name like Billy and is almost perfect,
But wears a stammer like a decoration:
And every time they meet the same thing has to happen;
It is the Evil that is helpless like a lover
And has to pick a quarrel and succeeds,
And both are openly destroyed before our eyes.

For now he was awake and knew
No one is ever spared except in dreams;
But there was something else the nightmare had distorted —
Even the punishment was human and a form of love:
The howling storm had been his father's presence
And all the time he had been carried on his father's breast.
Who now had set him gently down and left him.
He stood upon the narrow balcony and listened:
And all the stars above him sang as in his childhood
'All, all is vanity,' but it was not the same;
For now the words descended like the calm of mountains —
— Nathaniel had been shy because his love was selfish —
Reborn, he cried in exultation and surrender
'The Godhead is broken like bread. We are the pieces.'

And sat down at his desk and wrote a story.

The Unknown Citizen

(*To JS/07/M/378
This Marble Monument
Is Erected by the State*

He was found by the Bureau of Statistics to be
One against whom there was no official complaint,
And all the reports on his conduct agree
That, in the modern sense of an old-fashioned word, he was a
          saint,
For in everything he did he served the Greater Community.

Except for the War till the day he retired
He worked in a factory and never got fired,
But satisfied his employers, Fudge Motors Inc.
Yet he wasn't a scab or odd in his views,
For his Union reports that he paid his dues,
(Our report on his Union shows it was sound)
And our Social Psychology workers found
That he was popular with his mates and liked a drink.
The Press are convinced that he bought a paper every day
And that his reactions to advertisements were normal in every
     way.
Policies taken out in his name prove that he was fully insured,
And his Health-card shows he was once in hospital but left it
     cured.
Both Producers Research and High-Grade Living declare
He was fully sensible to the advantages of the Instalment Plan
And had everything necessary to the Modern Man,
A phonograph, a radio, a car and a frigidaire.
Our researchers into Public Opinion are content
That he held the proper opinions for the time of year;
When there was peace, he was for peace; when there was war,
     he went.
He was married and added five children to the population,
Which our Eugenist says was the right number for a parent of
     his generation,
And our teachers report that he never interfered with their
     education.
Was he free? Was he happy? The question is absurd:
Had anything been wrong, we should certainly have heard.

The Prophets

Perhaps I always knew what they were saying:
Even those earliest messengers who walked
Into my life from books where they were staying,
Those beautiful machines that never talked
But let the small boy worship them and learn
All their long names whose hardness made him proud;

147

Love was the word they never said aloud
As nothing that a picture can return.

And later when I hunted the Good Place,
Abandoned lead-mines let themselves be caught;
There was no pity in the adit's face,
The rusty winding-engine never taught
One obviously too apt, to say Too Late:
Their lack of shyness was a way of praising
Just what I didn't know, why I was gazing,
While all their lack of answer whispered 'Wait,'
And taught me gradually without coercion,
And all the landscape round them pointed to
The calm with which they took complete desertion
As proof that you existed.

                    It was true.
For now I have the answer from the face
That never will go back into a book
But asks for all my life, and is the Place
Where all I touch is moved to an embrace,
And there is no such thing as a vain look.

Like a Vocation

Not as that dream Napoleon, rumour's dread and centre,
Before whose riding all the crowds divide,
Who dedicates a column and withdraws,
Nor as that general favourite and breezy visitor
To whom the weather and the ruins mean so much,
Nor as any of those who always will be welcome,
As luck or history or fun,
Do not enter like that: all these depart.

Claim, certainly, the stranger's right to pleasure:
Ambassadors will surely entertain you
With knowledge of operas and men,
Bankers will ask for your opinion

And the heiress' cheek lean ever so slightly towards you,
The mountains and the shopkeepers accept you
And all your walks be free.

But politeness and freedom are never enough,
Not for a life. They lead
Up to a bed that only looks like marriage;
Even the disciplined and distant admiration
For thousands who obviously want nothing
Becomes just a dowdy illness. These have their moderate success;
They exist in the vanishing hour.

But somewhere always, nowhere particularly unusual,
Almost anywhere in the landscape of water and houses,
His crying competing unsuccessfully with the cry
Of the traffic or the birds, is always standing
The one who needs you, that terrified
Imaginative child who only knows you
As what the uncles call a lie,
But knows he has to be the future and that only
The meek inherit the earth, and is neither
Charming, successful, nor a crowd;
Alone among the noise and policies of summer,
His weeping climbs towards your life like a vocation.

The Riddle

Underneath the leaves of life,
Green on the prodigious tree,
    In a trance of grief
Stand the fallen man and wife:
Far away a single stag
Banished to a lonely crag
Gazes placid out to sea,
While from thickets round about
Breeding animals look in
    On Duality,
And small birds fly in and out
    Of the world of man.

Down in order from a ridge,
Bayonets glittering in the sun,
    Soldiers who will judge
Wind towards a little bridge:
Even orators may speak
Truths of value to the weak,
Necessary acts are done
By the ill and the unjust;
But the Judgment and the Smile,
    Though these two-in-one
See creation as they must,
    None shall reconcile.

Bordering our middle earth
Kingdoms of the Short and Tall,
    Rivals for our faith,
Stir up envy from our birth:
So the giant who storms the sky
In an angry wish to die
Wakes the hero in us all,
While the tiny with their power
To divide and hide and flee,
    When our fortunes fall,
Tempt to a belief in our
    Immortality.

Lovers running each to each
Feel such timid dreams catch fire
    Blazing as they touch,
Learn what love alone can teach:
Happy on a tousled bed
Praise Blake's acumen who said:
'One thing only we require
Of each other; we must see
In another's lineaments
    Gratified desire';
That is our humanity;
    Nothing else contents.

Nowhere else could I have known
Than, beloved, in your eyes
    What we have to learn,
That we love ourselves alone:
All our terrors burned away
We can learn at last to say:
'All our knowledge comes to this,
That existence is enough,
That in savage solitude
    Or the play of love
Every living creature is
    Woman, Man, and Child'.

Heavy Date

Sharp and silent in the
Clear October lighting
Of a Sunday morning
    The great city lies;
And I at a window
Looking over water
At the world of Business
    With a lover's eyes.

All mankind, I fancy,
When anticipating
Anything exciting
    Like a rendezvous,
Occupy the time in
Purely random thinking,
For when love is waiting
    Logic will not do.

Much as he would like to
Concentrate completely
On the precious Object,
    Love has not the power:

151

Goethe put it neatly;
No one cares to watch the
Loveliest sunset after
    Quarter of an hour.

Malinowski, Rivers,
Benedict and others
Show how common culture
    Shapes the separate lives:
Matrilineal races
Kill their mothers' brothers
In their dreams and turn their
    Sisters into wives.

Who when looking over
Faces in the subway,
Each with its uniqueness,
    Would not, did he dare,
Ask what forms exactly
Suited to their weakness
Love and desperation
    Take to govern there:

Would not like to know what
Influence occupation
Has on human vision
    Of the human fate:
Do all clerks for instance
Pigeon-hole creation,
Brokers see the Ding-an-
    -sich as Real Estate?

When a politician
Dreams about his sweetheart,
Does he multiply her
    Face into a crowd,
Are her fond responses
All-or-none reactions,
Does he try to buy her,
    Is the kissing loud?

Strange are love's mutations:
Thus, the early poem
Of the flesh sub rosa
   Has been known to grow
Now and then into the
Amor intellectu-
-alis of Spinoza;
   How we do not know.

Slowly we are learning,
We at least know this much,
That we have to unlearn
   Much that we were taught,
And are growing chary
Of emphatic dogmas;
Love like Matter is much
   Odder than we thought.

Love requires an Object,
But this varies so much,
Almost, I imagine,
   Anything will do:
When I was a child, I
Loved a pumping-engine,
Thought it every bit as
   Beautiful as you.

Love has no position,
Love's a way of living,
One kind of relation
   Possible between
Any things or persons
Given one condition,
The one sine qua non
   Being mutual need.

Through it we discover
An essential secret
Called by some Salvation
   And by some Success;

Crying for the moon is
Naughtiness and envy,
We can only love what-
-ever we possess.

I believed for years that
Love was the conjunction
Of two oppositions;
  That was all untrue;
Every young man fears that
He is not worth loving:
Bless you, darling, I have
  Found myself in you.

When two lovers meet, then
There's an end of writing
Thought and Analytics:
  Lovers, like the dead,
In their loves are equal;
Sophomores and peasants,
Poets and their critics
  Are the same in bed.

Law Like Love

Law, say the gardeners, is the sun,
Law is the one
All gardeners obey
To-morrow, yesterday, to-day.

Law is the wisdom of the old,
The impotent grandfathers feebly scold;
The grandchildren put out a treble tongue,
Law is the senses of the young.

Law, says the priest with a priestly look,
Expounding to an unpriestly people,
Law is the words in my priestly book,
Law is my pulpit and my steeple.

Law, says the judge as he looks down his nose,
Speaking clearly and most severely,
Law is as I've told you before,
Law is as you know I suppose,
Law is but let me explain it once more,
Law is The Law.

Yet law-abiding scholars write:
Law is neither wrong nor right,
Law is only crimes
Punished by places and by times,
Law is the clothes men wear
Anytime, anywhere,
Law is Good morning and Good night.

Others say, Law is our Fate;
Others say, Law is our State;
Others say, others say
Law is no more,
Law has gone away.

And always the loud angry crowd,
Very angry and very loud,
Law is We,
And always the soft idiot softly Me.

If we, dear, know we know no more
Than they about the Law,
If I no more than you
Know what we should and should not do
Except that all agree
Gladly or miserably
That the Law is
And that all know this,
If therefore thinking it absurd
To identify Law with some other word,
Unlike so many men
I cannot say Law is again,

No more than they can we suppress
The universal wish to guess
Or slip out of our own position
Into an unconcerned condition.
Although I can at least confine
Your vanity and mine
To stating timidly
A timid similarity,
We shall boast anyway:
Like love I say.

Like love we don't know where or why,
Like love we can't compel or fly,
Like love we often weep,
Like love we seldom keep.

The Hidden Law

The Hidden Law does not deny
Our laws of probability,
But takes the atom and the star
And human beings as they are,
And answers nothing when we lie.

It is the only reason why
No government can codify,
And legal definitions mar
    The Hidden Law.

Its utter patience will not try
To stop us if we want to die:
When we escape It in a car,
When we forget It in a bar,
These are the ways we're punished by
    The Hidden Law.

Twelve Songs

I

Say this city has ten million souls,
Some are living in mansions, some are living in holes:
Yet there's no place for us, my dear, yet there's no place for us.

Once we had a country and we thought it fair,
Look in the atlas and you'll find it there:
We cannot go there now, my dear, we cannot go there now.

In the village churchyard there grows an old yew,
Every spring it blossoms anew:
Old passports can't do that, my dear, old passports can't do that.

The consul banged the table and said:
'If you've got no passport you're officially dead':
But we are still alive, my dear, but we are still alive.

Went to a committee; they offered me a chair;
Asked me politely to return next year:
But where shall we go to-day, my dear, but where shall we go
      to-day?

Came to a public meeting; the speaker got up and said:
'If we let them in, they will steal our daily bread';
He was talking of you and me, my dear, he was talking of you
      and me.

Thought I heard the thunder rumbling in the sky;
It was Hitler over Europe, saying: 'They must die';
We were in his mind, my dear, we were in his mind.

Saw a poodle in a jacket fastened with a pin,
Saw a door opened and a cat let in:
But they weren't German Jews, my dear, but they weren't
      German Jews.

Went down the harbour and stood upon the quay,
Saw the fish swimming as if they were free:
Only ten feet away, my dear, only ten feet away.

Walked through a wood, saw the birds in the trees;
They had no politicians and sang at their ease:
They weren't the human race, my dear, they weren't the
    human race.

Dreamed I saw a building with a thousand floors,
A thousand windows and a thousand doors;
Not one of them was ours, my dear, not one of them was ours.

Stood on a great plain in the falling snow;
Ten thousand soldiers marched to and fro:
Looking for you and me, my dear, looking for you and me.

II. (CALYPSO)

Dríver, drive fáster and máke a good rún
Dówn the Spríngfield Line únder the shíning sún.

Flý like an áeroplane, dón't pull up shórt
Till you bráke for Grand Céntral Státion, New Yórk.

For thére in the míddle of thát waiting-háll
Should be stánding the óne that Í love best of áll.

If he's nót there to méet me when Í get to tówn,
I'll stánd on the síde-walk with téars rolling dówn.

For he ís the óne that I lóve to look ón,
The ácme of kíndness and perféction.

He présses my hánd and he sáys he loves mé,
Which I fínd an admírable pecúliarity.

The woods are bright green on both sides of the line;
The trees have their loves though they're different from mine.

But the poor fat old banker in the sun-parlor car
Has no one to love him except his cigar.

If I were the Head of the Church or the State,
I'd powder my nose and just tell them to wait.

For love's more important and powerful than
Even a priest or a politician.

III

Warm are the still and lucky miles,
White shores of longing stretch away,
A light of recognition fills
    The whole great day, and bright
The tiny world of lovers' arms.

Silence invades the breathing wood
Where drowsy limbs a treasure keep,
Now greenly falls the learned shade
    Across the sleeping brows
And stirs their secret to a smile.

Restored! Returned! The lost are borne
On seas of shipwreck home at last:
See! In a fire of praising burns
    The dry dumb past, and we
Our life-day long shall part no more.

IV

Carry her over the water,
　And set her down under the tree,
Where the culvers white all day and all night,
　And the winds from every quarter,
Sing agreeably, agreeably, agreeably of love.

Put a gold ring on her finger,
　And press her close to your heart,
While the fish in the lake their snapshots take,
　And the frog, that sanguine singer,
Sings agreeably, agreeably, agreeably of love.

The streets shall all flock to your marriage,
　The houses turn round to look,
The tables and chairs say suitable prayers,
　And the horses drawing your carriage
Sing agreeably, agreeably, agreeably of love.

V

Dog　The single creature leads a partial life,
　　　Man by his mind, and by his nose the hound;
　　　He needs the deep emotions I can give,
　　　I scent in him a vaster hunting ground.

Cats　Like calls to like, to share is to relieve
　　　And sympathy the root bears love the flower;
　　　He feels in us, and we in him perceive
　　　A common passion for the lonely hour.

Cats　We move in our apartness and our pride
　　　About the decent dwellings he has made:
Dog　In all his walks I follow at his side,
　　　His faithful servant and his loving shade.

VI

Eyes look into the well,
Tears run down from the eye;
The tower cracked and fell
From the quiet winter sky.

Under a midnight stone
Love was buried by thieves;
The robbed heart begs for a bone,
The damned rustle like leaves.

Face down in the flooded brook
With nothing more to say,
Lies One the soldiers took,
And spoiled and threw away.

VII

Jumbled in one common box
Of their dark stupidity,
Orchid, swan, and Caesar lie;
Time that tires of everyone
Has corroded all the locks
Thrown away the key for fun.

In its cleft the torrent mocks
Prophets who in days gone by
Made a profit on each cry,
Persona grata now with none;
And a jackass language shocks
Poets who can only pun.

Silence settles on the clocks;
Nursing mothers point a sly
Index finger at a sky,
Crimson in the setting sun;
In the valley of the fox
Gleams the barrel of a gun.

Once we could have made the docks,
Now it is too late to fly;
Once too often you and I
Did what we should not have done;
Round the rampant rugged rocks
Rude and ragged rascals run.

VIII

Though determined Nature can
Only offer human eyes
One alternative to sleep,
Opportunity to weep,
   Who can refuse her?
Error does not end with youth
But increases in the man;
   All truth, only truth,
Carries the ambiguous lies
   Of the Accuser.

Though some sudden fire of grace
Visit our mortality
Till a whole life tremble for
Swans upon a river or
   Some passing stranger,
Hearts by envy are possessed
From the moment that they praise;
   To rejoice, to be blessed,
Places us immediately
   In mortal danger

Though we cannot follow how
Evil miracles are done
Through the medium of a kiss,
Aphrodite's garden is
   A haunted region;
For the very signs whereby
Lovers register their vow,
   With a look, with a sigh,

Summon to their meetings One
　　Whose name is Legion.

We, my darling, for our sins
Suffer in each other's woe,
Read in injured eyes and hands
How we broke divine commands
　　And served the Devil.
Who is passionate enough
When the punishment begins?
　　O my love, O my love,
In the night of fire and snow
　　Save me from evil.

IX

My second thoughts condemn
And wonder how I dare
To look you in the eye.
What right have I to swear
Even at one a.m.
To love you till I die?

Earth meets too many crimes
For fibs to interest her;
If I can give my word,
Forgiveness can recur
Any number of times
In Time. Which is absurd.

Tempus fugit. Quite.
So finish up your drink.
All flesh is grass. It is.
But who on earth can think
With heavy heart or light
Of what will come of this?

X

On and on and on
The forthright catadoup
Shouts at the stone-deaf stone;
Over and over again,
Singly or as a group,
Weak diplomatic men
With a small defiant light
Salute the incumbent night.

With or without a mind,
Chafant or outwardly calm,
Each thing has an axe to grind
And exclaims its matter-of-fact;
The child with careful charm
Or a sudden opprobrious act,
The tiger, the griping fern,
Extort the world's concern.

All, all, have rights to declare,
Not one is man enough
To be, simply, publicly, there
With no private emphasis;
So my embodied love
Which, like most feeling, is
Half humbug and half true,
Asks neighbourhood of you.

XI

Sing, Ariel, sing,
Sweetly, dangerously
Out of the sour
And shiftless water,
Lucidly out
Of the dozing tree,
Entrancing, rebuking
The raging heart

With a smoother song
Than this rough world,
Unfeeling god.

O brilliantly, lightly,
Of separation,
Of bodies and death,
Unanxious one, sing
To man, meaning me,
As now, meaning always,
In love or out,
Whatever that mean,
Trembling he takes
The silent passage
Into discomfort.

XII

When the Sex War ended with the slaughter of the Grandmothers,
They found a bachelor's baby suffocating under them;
Somebody called him George and that was the end of it;
   They hitched him up to the Army.
   George, you old debutante,
   How did you get in the Army?

In the Retreat from Reason he deserted on his rocking-horse
And lived on a fairy's kindness till he tired of kicking her;
He smashed her spectacles and stole her cheque-book and
    mackintosh
   Then cruised his way back to the Army.
   George, you old numero,
   How did you get in the Army?

Before the Diet of Sugar he was using razor-blades
And exited soon after with an allergy to maidenheads;
He discovered a cure of his own, but no one would patent it,
   So he showed up again in the Army.
   George, you old flybynight,
   How did you get in the Army?

When the Vice Crusades were over he was hired by some
    Muscovites
Prospecting for deodorants among the Eskimos;
He was caught by a common cold and condemned to the whiskey
    mines,
    But schemozzled back to the Army.
    George, you old Emperor,
    How did you get in the Army?

Since Peace was signed with Honour he's been minding his
    business;
But, whoops, here comes His Idleness, buttoning his uniform;
Just in tidy time to massacre the Innocents;
    He's come home to roost in the Army.
    George, you old matador,
    Welcome back to the Army.

In Memory of Sigmund Freud

(d. Sept. 1939)

When there are so many we shall have to mourn,
when grief has been made so public, and exposed
    to the critique of a whole epoch
    the frailty of our conscience and anguish,

of whom shall we speak? For every day they die
among us, those who were doing us some good,
    who knew it was never enough but
    hoped to improve a little by living.

Such was this doctor: still at eighty he wished
to think of our life from whose unruliness
    so many plausible young futures
    with threats or flattery ask obedience,

166

but his wish was denied him: he closed his eyes
upon that last picture, common to us all,
    of problems like relatives gathered
   puzzled and jealous about our dying.

For about him till the very end were still
those he had studied, the fauna of the night,
    and shades that still waited to enter
   the bright circle of his recognition

turned elsewhere with their disappointment as he
was taken away from his life interest
    to go back to the earth in London,
   an important Jew who died in exile.

Only Hate was happy, hoping to augment
his practice now, and his dingy clientele
    who think they can be cured by killing
   and covering the gardens with ashes.

They are still alive, but in a world he changed
simply by looking back with no false regrets;
    all he did was to remember
   like the old and be honest like children.

He wasn't clever at all: he merely told
the unhappy Present to recite the Past
    like a poetry lesson till sooner
   or later it faltered at the line where

long ago the accusations had begun,
and suddenly knew by whom it had been judged,
    how rich life had been and how silly,
   and was life-forgiven and more humble,

able to approach the Future as a friend
without a wardrobe of excuses, without
    a set mask of rectitude or an
   embarrassing over-familiar gesture.

No wonder the ancient cultures of conceit
in his technique of unsettlement foresaw
    the fall of princes, the collapse of
  their lucrative patterns of frustration:

if he succeeded, why, the Generalised Life
would become impossible, the monolith
    of State be broken and prevented
  the co-operation of avengers.

Of course they called on God, but he went his way
down among the lost people like Dante, down
    to the stinking fosse where the injured
  lead the ugly life of the rejected,

and showed us what evil is, not, as we thought,
deeds that must be punished, but our lack of faith,
    our dishonest mood of denial,
  the concupiscence of the oppressor.

If some traces of the autocratic pose,
the paternal strictness he distrusted, still
    clung to his utterance and features,
  it was a protective coloration

for one who'd lived among enemies so long:
if often he was wrong and, at times, absurd,
    to us he is no more a person
  now but a whole climate of opinion

under whom we conduct our different lives:
Like weather he can only hinder or help,
    the proud can still be proud but find it
  a little harder, the tyrant tries to

make do with him but doesn't care for him much:
he quietly surrounds all our habits of growth
    and extends, till the tired in even
  the remotest miserable duchy

have felt the change in their bones and are cheered,
till the child, unlucky in his little State,
    some hearth where freedom is excluded,
  a hive whose honey is fear and worry,

feels calmer now and somehow assured of escape,
while, as they lie in the grass of our neglect,
    so many long-forgotten objects
  revealed by his undiscouraged shining

are returned to us and made precious again;
games we had thought we must drop as we grew up,
    little noises we dared not laugh at,
  faces we made when no one was looking.

But he wishes us more than this. To be free
is often to be lonely. He would unite
    the unequal moieties fractured
  by our own well-meaning sense of justice,

would restore to the larger the wit and will
the smaller possesses but can only use
    for arid disputes, would give back to
  the son the mother's richness of feeling:

but he would have us remember most of all
to be enthusiastic over the night,
    not only for the sense of wonder
  it alone has to offer, but also

because it needs our love. With large sad eyes
its delectable creatures look up and beg
    us dumbly to ask them to follow:
  they are exiles who long for the future

that lies in our power, they too would rejoice
if allowed to serve enlightenment like him,
    even to bear our cry of 'Judas',
  as he did and all must bear who serve it.

One rational voice is dumb. Over his grave
the household of Impulse mourns one dearly loved:
    sad is Eros, builder of cities,
    and weeping anarchic Aphrodite.

Another Time

For us like any other fugitive,
Like the numberless flowers that cannot number
And all the beasts that need not remember,
It is to-day in which we live.

So many try to say Not Now,
So many have forgotten how
To say I Am, and would be
Lost, if they could, in history.

Bowing, for instance, with such old-world grace
To a proper flag in a proper place,
Muttering like ancients as they stump upstairs
Of Mine and His or Ours and Theirs.

Just as if time were what they used to will
When it was gifted with possession still,
Just as if they were wrong
In no more wishing to belong.

No wonder then so many die of grief,
So many are so lonely as they die;
No one has yet believed or liked a lie:
Another time has other lives to live.

Our Bias

The hour-glass whispers to the lion's roar,
The clock-towers tell the gardens day and night
How many errors Time has patience for,
How wrong they are in being always right.

Yet Time, however loud its chimes or deep,
However fast its falling torrent flows,
Has never put one lion off his leap
Nor shaken the assurance of a rose.

For they, it seems, care only for success:
While we choose words according to their sound
And judge a problem by its awkwardness;

And Time with us was always popular.
When have we not preferred some going round
To going straight to where we are?

Hell

Hell is neither here nor there,
Hell is not anywhere,
Hell is hard to bear.

It is so hard to dream posterity
Or haunt a ruined century
And so much easier to be.

Only the challenge to our will,
Our pride in learning any skill,
Sustains our effort to be ill.

To talk the dictionary through
Without a chance word coming true
Is more than Darwin's apes could do.

Yet pride alone could not insist
Did we not hope, if we persist,
That one day Hell might actually exist.

In time, pretending to be blind
And universally unkind
Might really send us out of our mind.

If we were really wretched and asleep
It would be then *de trop* to weep,
It would be natural to lie,
There'd be no living left to die.

Lady Weeping At The Crossroads

Lady, weeping at the crossroads,
Would you meet your love
In the twilight with his greyhounds,
And the hawk on his glove?

Bribe the birds then on the branches,
Bribe them to be dumb,
Stare the hot sun out of heaven
That the night may come.

Starless are the nights of travel,
Bleak the winter wind;
Run with terror all before you
And regret behind.

Run until you hear the ocean's
Everlasting cry;
Deep though it may be and bitter
You must drink it dry,

Wear out patience in the lowest
Dungeons of the sea,
Searching through the stranded shipwrecks
For the golden key,

Push on to the world's end, pay the
Dread guard with a kiss,
Cross the rotten bridge that totters
Over the abyss.

There stands the deserted castle
Ready to explore;
Enter, climb the marble staircase
Open the locked door.

Cross the silent empty ballroom,
Doubt and danger past;
Blow the cobwebs from the mirror
See yourself at last.

Put your hand behind the wainscot,
You have done your part;
Find the penknife there and plunge it
Into your false heart.

Anthem for St. Cecilia's Day

(for Benjamin Britten)

I

In a garden shady this holy lady
With reverent cadence and subtle psalm,
Like a black swan as death came on
Poured forth her song in perfect calm:
And by ocean's margin this innocent virgin
Constructed an organ to enlarge her prayer,
And notes tremendous from her great engine
Thundered out on the Roman air.

Blonde Aphrodite rose up excited,
Moved to delight by the melody,

173

White as an orchid she rode quite naked
In an oyster shell on top of the sea;
At sounds so entrancing the angels dancing
Came out of their trance into time again,
And around the wicked in Hell's abysses
The huge flame flickered and eased their pain.

Blessed Cecilia, appear in visions
To all musicians, appear and inspire:
Translated Daughter, come down and startle
Composing mortals with immortal fire.

II

I cannot grow;
I have no shadow
To run away from,
I only play.

I cannot err;
There is no creature
Whom I belong to,
Whom I could wrong.

I am defeat
When it knows it
Can now do nothing
By suffering.

All you lived through,
Dancing because you
No longer need it
For any deed.

I shall never be
Different. Love me.

III

O ear whose creatures cannot wish to fall,
Calm spaces unafraid of wear or weight,
Where Sorrow is herself, forgetting all
The gaucheness of her adolescent state,
Where Hope within the altogether strange
From every outworn image is released,
And Dread born whole and normal like a beast
Into a world of truths that never change:
Restore our fallen day; O re-arrange.

O dear white children casual as birds,
Playing among the ruined languages,
So small beside their large confusing words,
So gay against the greater silences
Of dreadful things you did: O hang the head,
Impetuous child with the tremendous brain,
O weep, child, weep, O weep away the stain,
Lost innocence who wished your lover dead,
Weep for the lives your wishes never led.

O cry created as the bow of sin
Is drawn across our trembling violin.
O weep, child, weep, O weep away the stain.
O law drummed out by hearts against the still
Long winter of our intellectual will.
That what has been may never be again.
O flute that throbs with the thanksgiving breath
Of convalescents on the shores of death.
O bless the freedom that you never chose.
O trumpets that unguarded children blow
About the fortress of their inner foe.
O wear your tribulation like a rose.

The Dark Years

Returning each morning from a timeless world,
the senses open upon a world of time:
    after so many years the light is
    novel still and immensely ambitious,

but, translated from her own informal world,
the ego is bewildered and does not want
    a shining novelty this morning,
    and does not like the noise or the people.

For behind the doors of this ambitious day
stand shadows with enormous grudges, outside
    its chartered ocean of perception
    misshapen coastguards drunk with foreboding,

and whispering websters, creeping through this world,
discredit so much literature and praise.
    Summer was worse than we expected:
    now an Autumn cold comes on the water,

as lesser lives retire on their savings, their
small deposits of starches and nuts, and soon
    will be asleep or travelling
    or dead. But this year the towns of our childhood

are changing complexion along with the woods,
and many who have shared our conduct will add
    their pinches of detritus to the
    nutritive chain of determined being,

and even our uneliminated decline
to a vita minima, huddling for warmth,
    the hard- and the soft-mouthed together
    in a coma of waiting, just breathing

in a darkness of tribulation and death,
while blizzards havoc the garden and the old
    Folly becomes unsafe, the mill-wheels
    rust, and the weirs fall slowly to pieces.

Will the inflamed ego attempt as before
to migrate again to her family place,
        to the hanging gardens of Eros
    and the moons of a magical summer?

The local train does not run any more,
the heretical roses have lost their scent,
        and her Cornish Hollow of tryst is
    swarming now with discourteous villains

whom Father's battered hat cannot wave away,
and the fancy-governed sequence leads us all
        back to the labyrinth where either
    we are found or lose ourselves for ever.

What signs ought we to make to be found, how can
we will the knowledge that we must know to will?
        The waste is a suburb of prophets,
    but who has seen Jesus and who only

Judas the Abyss? The rocks are big and bad,
death all too substantial in the thinning air,
        learning screams in the narrow gate where
    events are traded with time but cannot

tell what logic must and must not leave to fate,
or what laws we are permitted to obey:
        there are no birds now, predatory
    glaciers glitter in a chilly evening,

and death is probable. Nevertheless,
whatever the situation and the blame,
        let the lips make formal contrition
    for whatever is going to happen,

time remembered bear witness to time required,
the positive and negative ways through time
        embrace and encourage each other
    in a brief moment of intersection,

that the spirit orgulous may while it can
conform to its temporal focus with praise,
acknowledging the attributes of
one immortal, one infinite Substance,

and the shabby structure of indolent flesh
give a resonant echo to the Word which was
from the beginning, and the shining
Light be comprehended by the darkness.

The Quest

I

Out of it steps our future, through this door
Enigmas, executioners and rules,
Her Majesty in a bad temper or
A red-nosed Fool who makes a fool of fools.

Great persons eye it in the twilight for
A past it might so carelessly let in,
A widow with a missionary grin,
The foaming inundation at a roar.

We pile our all against it when afraid,
And beat upon its panels when we die:
By happening to be open once, it made

Enormous Alice see a wonderland
That waited for her in the sunshine and,
Simply by being tiny, made her cry.

II

All had been ordered weeks before the start
From the best firms at such work, instruments
To take the measure of all queer events,
And drugs to move the bowels or the heart.

A watch, of course, to watch impatience fly,
Lamps for the dark and shades against the sun;
Foreboding, too, insisted on a gun,
And coloured beads to soothe a savage eye.

In theory they were sound on Expectation,
Had there been situations to be in;
Unluckily they were their situation:

One should not give a poisoner medicine,
A conjurer fine apparatus, nor
A rifle to a melancholic bore.

III

Two friends who met here and embraced are gone,
Each to his own mistake; one flashes on
To fame and ruin in a rowdy lie,
A village torpor holds the other one,
Some local wrong where it takes time to die:
This empty junction glitters in the sun.

So at all quays and crossroads: who can tell
These places of decision and farewell
To what dishonour all adventure leads,
What parting gift could give that friend protection,
So orientated his vocation needs
The Bad Lands and the sinister direction?

All landscapes and all weathers freeze with fear,
But none have ever thought, the legends say,
The time allowed made it impossible;
For even the most pessimistic set
The limit of their errors at a year.
What friends could there be left then to betray,
What joy take longer to atone for; yet
Who would complete without the extra day
The journey that should take no time at all?

IV

No window in his suburb lights that bedroom where
A little fever heard large afternoons at play:
His meadows multiply; that mill, though, is not there
Which went on grinding at the back of love all day.

Nor all his weeping ways through weary wastes have found
The castle where his Greater Hallows are interned;
For broken bridges halt him, and dark thickets round
Some ruin where an evil heritage was burned.

Could he forget a child's ambition to be old
And institutions where it learned to wash and lie,
He'd tell the truth for which he thinks himself too young,

That everywhere on his horizon, all the sky,
Is now, as always, only waiting to be told
To be his father's house and speak his mother tongue.

V

In villages from which their childhoods came
Seeking Necessity, they had been taught
Necessity by nature is the same
No matter how or by whom it be sought.

The city, though, assumed no such belief,
But welcomed each as if he came alone,
The nature of Necessity like grief
Exactly corresponding to his own.

And offered them so many, every one
Found some temptation fit to govern him,
And settled down to master the whole craft

Of being nobody; sat in the sun
During the lunch-hour round the fountain rim,
And watched the country kids arrive and laughed.

VI

Ashamed to be the darling of his grief,
He joined a gang of rowdy stories where
His gift for magic quickly made him chief
Of all these boyish powers of the air;

Who turned his hungers into Roman food,
The town's asymmetry into a park;
All hours took taxis; any solitude
Became his flattered duchess in the dark.

But, if he wished for anything less grand,
The nights came padding after him like wild
Beasts that meant harm, and all the doors cried Thief;

And when Truth met him and put out her hand,
He clung in panic to his tall belief
And shrank away like an ill-treated child.

VII

His library annoyed him with its look
Of calm belief in being really there;
He threw away a rival's boring book,
And clattered panting up the spiral stair.

Swaying upon the parapet he cried:
'O Uncreated Nothing, set me free,
Now let Thy perfect be identified
Unending passion of the Night, with Thee.'

And his long-suffering flesh, that all the time
Had felt the simple cravings of the stone
And hoped to be rewarded for her climb,

Took it to be a promise when he spoke
That now at last she would be left alone,
And plunged into the college quad, and broke.

VIII

He watched with all his organs of concern
How princes walk, what wives and children say,
Re-opened old graves in his heart to learn
What laws the dead had died to disobey,

And came reluctantly to his conclusion:
'All the arm-chair philosophies are false;
To love another adds to the confusion;
The song of mercy is the Devil's Waltz.'

All that he put his hand to prospered so
That soon he was the very King of creatures,
Yet, in an autumn nightmare trembled, for,

Approaching down a ruined corridor,
Strode someone with his own distorted features
Who wept, and grew enormous, and cried Woe.

IX

This is an architecture for the odd;
Thus heaven was attacked by the afraid,
So once, unconsciously, a virgin made
Her maidenhead conspicuous to a god.

Here on dark nights while worlds of triumph sleep
Lost Love in abstract speculation burns,
And exiled Will to politics returns
In epic verse that makes its traitors weep.

Yet many come to wish their tower a well;
For those who dread to drown, of thirst may die,
Those who see all become invisible:

Here great magicians, caught in their own spell,
Long for a natural climate as they sigh
'Beware of Magic' to the passer-by.

X

They noticed that virginity was needed
To trap the unicorn in every case,
But not that, of those virgins who succeeded,
A high percentage had an ugly face.

The hero was as daring as they thought him,
But his peculiar boyhood missed them all;
The angel of a broken leg had taught him
The right precautions to avoid a fall.

So in presumption they set forth alone
On what, for them, was not compulsory,
And stuck half-way to settle in some cave
With desert lions to domesticity,

Or turned aside to be absurdly brave,
And met the ogre and were turned to stone.

XI

His peasant parents killed themselves with toil
To let their darling leave a stingy soil
For any of those fine professions which
Encourage shallow breathing, and grow rich.

The pressure of their fond ambition made
Their shy and country-loving child afraid
No sensible career was good enough,
Only a hero could deserve such love.

So here he was without maps or supplies,
A hundred miles from any decent town;
The desert glared into his blood-shot eyes,
The silence roared displeasure:
                                    looking down,
He saw the shadow of an Average Man
Attempting the exceptional, and ran.

XII

Incredulous, he stared at the amused
Official writing down his name among
Those whose request to suffer was refused.

The pen ceased scratching: though he came too late
To join the martyrs, there was still a place
Among the tempters for a caustic tongue

To test the resolution of the young
With tales of the small failings of the great,
And shame the eager with ironic praise.

Though mirrors might be hateful for a while,
Women and books would teach his middle age
The fencing wit of an informal style,
To keep the silences at bay and cage
His pacing manias in a worldly smile.

XIII

The over-logical fell for the witch
Whose argument converted him to stone,
Thieves rapidly absorbed the over-rich,
The over-popular went mad alone,
And kisses brutalized the over-male.

As agents their importance quickly ceased;
Yet, in proportion as they seemed to fail,
Their instrumental value was increased
For one predestined to attain their wish.

By standing stones the blind can feel their way,
Wild dogs compel the cowardly to fight,
Beggars assist the slow to travel light,
And even madmen manage to convey
Unwelcome truths in lonely gibberish.

XIV

Fresh addenda are published every day
To the encyclopedia of the Way,

Linguistic notes and scientific explanations,
And texts for schools with modernized spelling and illustrations.

Now everyone knows the hero must choose the old horse,
Abstain from liquor and sexual intercourse,

And look out for a stranded fish to be kind to:
Now everyone thinks he could find, had he a mind to,

The way through the waste to the chapel in the rock
For a vision of the Triple Rainbow or the Astral Clock,

Forgetting his information comes mostly from married men
Who liked fishing and a flutter on the horses now and then.

And how reliable can any truth be that is got
By observing oneself and then just inserting a Not?

XV

Suppose he'd listened to the erudite committee,
He would have only found where not to look;
Suppose his terrier when he whistled had obeyed,
It would not have unearthed the buried city;
Suppose he had dismissed the careless maid,
The cryptogram would not have fluttered from the book.

'I was not I,' he cried as, healthy and astounded,
He stepped across a predecessor's skull;
'A nonsense jingle simply came into my head
And left the intellectual Sphinx dumbfounded;
I won the Queen because my hair was red;
The terrible adventure is a little dull.'

Hence Failure's torment: 'Was I doomed in any case,
Or would I not have failed had I believed in Grace?'

XVI

He parried every question that they hurled:
'What did the Emperor tell you?' 'Not to push?'
'What is the greatest wonder of the world?'
'The bare man Nothing in the Beggar's Bush.'

Some muttered; 'He is cagey for effect.
A hero owes a duty to his fame.
He looks too like a grocer for respect.'
Soon they slipped back into his Christian name.

The only difference that could be seen
From those who'd never risked their lives at all
Was his delight in details and routine:

For he was always glad to mow the grass,
Pour liquids from large bottles into small,
Or look at clouds through bits of coloured glass.

XVII

Others had found it prudent to withdraw
Before official pressure was applied,
Embittered robbers outlawed by the Law,
Lepers in terror of the terrified.

But no one else accused these of a crime;
They did not look ill: old friends, overcome,
Stared as they rolled away from talk and time
Like marbles out into the blank and dumb.

The crowd clung all the closer to convention,
Sunshine and horses, for the sane know why
The even numbers should ignore the odd:

The Nameless is what no free people mention;
Successful men know better than to try
To see the face of their Absconded God.

XVIII

Spinning upon their central thirst like tops,
They went the Negative Way towards the Dry;
By empty caves beneath an empty sky
They emptied out their memories like slops,

Which made a foul marsh as they dried to death,
Where monsters bred who forced them to forget
The lovelies their consent avoided; yet,
Still praising the Absurd with their last breath,

They seeded out into their miracles:
The images of each grotesque temptation
Became some painter's happiest inspiration,

And barren wives and burning virgins came
To drink the pure cold water of their wells,
And wish for beaux and children in their name.

XIX

Poet, oracle, and wit
Like unsuccessful anglers by
The ponds of apperception sit,
Baiting with the wrong request
The vectors of their interest,
At nightfall tell the angler's lie.

With time in tempest everywhere,
To rafts of frail assumption cling
The saintly and the insincere;
Enraged phenomena bear down
In overwhelming waves to drown
Both sufferer and suffering.

The waters long to hear our question put
Which would release their longed-for answer, but.

XX

Within these gates all opening begins:
White shouts and flickers through its green and red,
Where children play at seven earnest sins
And dogs believe their tall conditions dead.

Here adolescence into number breaks
The perfect circle time can draw on stone,
And flesh forgives division as it makes
Another's moment of consent its own.

All journeys die here: wish and weight are lifted:
Where often round some old maid's desolation
Roses have flung their glory like a cloak,

The gaunt and great, the famed for conversation
Blushed in the stare of evening as they spoke
And felt their centre of volition shifted.

Shorts

Motionless, deep in his mind, lies the past the poet's forgotten,
Till some small experience wake it to life and a poem's begotten,
Words its presumptive primordia, Feeling its field of induction,
Meaning its pattern of growth determined during construction.

* * *

Whether determined by God or their neural structure, still
All men have one common creed, account for it as you will:
The Truth is one and incapable of self-contradiction;
All knowledge that conflicts with itself is Poetic Fiction.

* * *

His ageing nature is the same
As when childhood wore its name
In an atmosphere of love,
And to itself appeared enough:

Only now, when he has come
In walking distance of his tomb,
He at last discovers who
He had always been to whom
He so often was untrue.

*   *   *

Babies in their mothers' arms
Exercise their budding charms
On their fingers and their toes,
Striving ever to enclose
In the circle of their will
Objects disobedient still,
But the boy comes fast enough
To the limits of self-love,
And the adult learns what small
Forces rally at his call.
Large and paramount the State
That will not co-operate
With the Duchy of his mind:
All his lifetime he will find
Swollen knee or aching tooth
Hostile to his quest for truth;
Never will his prick belong
To his world of right and wrong,
Nor its values comprehend
Who is foe and who is friend.

*   *   *

Do we want to return to the womb? Not at all.
No one really desires the impossible:
That is only the image out of our past
We practical people use when we cast
Our eyes on the future, to whom freedom is
The absence of all dualities.
Since there never can be much of that for us
In the universe of Copernicus,
Any heaven we think it decent to enter
Must be Ptolomaic with ourselves at the centre.

*   *   *

Once for candy Cook had stolen
    X was punished by Papa;
When he asked where babies come from,
    He was lied to by Mama.

Now the city streets are waiting
    To mislead him, and he must
Keep an eye on ageing beggars
    Lest they strike him in disgust.

* * *

With what conviction the young man spoke
When he thought his nonsense rather a joke;
Now, when he doesn't doubt any more,
No one believes the booming old bore.

* * *

To the man-in-the-street who, I'm sorry to say,
        Is a keen observer of life,
The word *intellectual* suggests right away
        A man who's untrue to his wife.

* * *

Base words are uttered only by the base
And can for such at once be understood,
But noble platitudes: — ah, there's a case
Where the most careful scrutiny is needed
To tell a voice that's genuinely good
From one that's base but merely has succeeded.

* * *

These public men who seem so to enjoy their dominion,
With their ruined faces and voices treble with hate,
Are no less martyrs because unaware of their fetters:
What would *you* be like, were you never allowed to create
Or reflect, but compelled to give an immediate opinion,
Condemned to destroy or distribute the works of your betters?

* * *

The Champion smiles — What Personality!
The Challenger scowls — How horrid he must be!
But let the Belt change hands and they change places,
Still from the same old corners come the same grimaces.

* * *

When Statesmen gravely say 'We must be realistic',
The chances are they're weak and, therefore, pacifistic,
But when they speak of Principles, look out: perhaps
Their generals are already poring over maps.

* * *

Who will cure the nation's ill?
A leader with a selfless will.
But how will you find this leader of yours?
By process of Natural Selection, of course.

* * *

Standing among the ruins, the horror-struck conqueror exclaimed:
'Why do they have to attempt to refuse me my destiny? Why?'

* * *

Why are the public buildings so high? How come you don't
    know?
Why, that's because the spirits of the public are so low.

* * *

'Hard cases make bad law', as the politician learns to his cost:
Yet just is the artist's reproach; 'Who generalises is lost.'

* * *

Don't you dream of a world, a society, with no coercion?
Yes: where a foetus is able to refuse to be born.

* * *

Hans-in-Kelder, Hans-in-Kelder,
    What are you waiting for?
We need your strong arm to look after the farm,
    And keep the wolf from the door.

191

Hans-in-Kelder, Hans-in-Kelder,
   Came out of the parsley-bed;
Came out at a run and levelled a gun
   And shot his old parents dead.

No Time

Clocks cannot tell our time of day
For what event to pray,
Because we have no time, because
We have no time until
We know what time we fill,
Why time is other than time was.

Nor can our question satisfy
The answer in the statue's eye.
Only the living ask whose brow
May wear the Roman laurel now:
The dead say only how.

What happens to the living when they die?
Death is not understood by death: nor you, nor I.

Diaspora

How he survived them they could never understand:
Had they not beggared him themselves to prove
They could not live without their dogmas or their land?

No worlds they drove him from were ever big enough:
How *could* it be the earth the Unconfined
Meant when It bade them set no limits to their love?

And he fulfilled the role for which he was designed:
On heat with fear, he drew their terrors to him,
And was a godsend to the lowest of mankind,

Till there was no place left where they could still pursue him
Except that exile which he called his race.
But, envying him even that, they plunged right through him

Into a land of mirrors without time or space,
And all they had to strike now was the human face.

Luther

With conscience cocked to listen for the thunder,
He saw the Devil busy in the wind,
Over the chiming steeples and then under
The doors of nuns and doctors who had sinned.

What apparatus could stave off disaster
Or cut the brambles of man's error down?
Flesh was a silent dog that bites its master,
World a still pond in which its children drown.

The fuse of Judgement spluttered in his head:
'Lord, smoke these honeyed insects from their hives.
All Works, Great Men, Societies are bad.
The Just shall live by Faith . . .' he cried in dread.

And men and women of the world were glad,
Who'd never cared or trembled in their lives.

Montaigne

Outside his library window he could see
A gentle landscape terrified of grammar,
Cities where lisping was compulsory,
And provinces where it was death to stammer.

The hefty sprawled, too tired to care: it took
This donnish undersexed conservative
To start a revolution and to give
The Flesh its weapons to defeat the Book.

When devils drive the reasonable wild,
They strip their adult century so bare,
Love must be re-grown from the sensual child,

To doubt becomes a way of definition,
Even belles lettres legitimate as prayer,
And laziness a movement of contrition.

The Council

In gorgeous robes befitting the occasion,
For weeks their spiritual and temporal lordships met
To reconcile eternity with time and set
Our earth of marriage on a sure foundation.
The little town was full of spies: corrupt mankind
Waited on tenterhooks.

                   With ostentation
Doors were at last flung back; success had been complete:
The formulae essential to salvation
Were phrased for ever and the true relation
Of Agape to Eros finally defined.
The burghers hung out flags in celebration;
The peasants danced and roasted oxen in the street.

Into their joy four heralds galloped up with news.
'Fierce tribes are moving on the Western Marches.
Out East a virgin has conceived a son again.
The Southern shipping-lanes are in the hands of Jews.
The Northern Provinces are much deluded
By one who claims there are not seven stars but ten.'

Who wrote upon the council-chamber arches
That sad exasperated cry of tired old men:
Postremum Sanctus Spiritus effudit?

The Maze

Anthropos apteros for days
Walked whistling round and round the maze,
Relying happily upon
His temperament for getting on.

The hundredth time he sighted, though,
A bush he left an hour ago,
He halted where four alleys crossed
And recognised that he was lost.

'Where am I? Metaphysics says
No question can be asked unless
It has an answer, so I can
Assume this maze has got a plan.

'If theologians are correct,
A Plan implies an Architect:
A God-built maze would be, I'm sure,
The Universe in miniature.

'Are data from the world of sense,
In that case, valid evidence?
What, in the universe I know,
Can give directions how to go?

'All Mathematics would suggest
A steady straight line as the best,
But left and right alternately
Is consonant with History.

'Aesthetics, though, believes all Art
Intends to gratify the heart:
Rejecting disciplines like these,
Must I, then, go which way I please?

'Such reasoning is only true
If we accept the classic view,
Which we have no right to assert
According to the introvert.

'His absolute presupposition
Is: Man creates his own condition.
This maze was not divinely built
But is secreted by my guilt.

'The centre that I cannot find
Is known to my unconscious mind;
I have no reason to despair
Because I am already there.

'My problem is how not to will;
They move most quickly who stand still:
I'm only lost until I see
I'm lost because I want to be.

'If this should fail, perhaps I should,
As certain educators would,
Content myself with this conclusion:
In theory there is no solution.

'All statements about what I feel,
Like I-am-lost, are quite unreal:
My knowledge ends where it began;
A hedge is taller than a man.'

Anthropos apteros, perplexed
To know which turning to take next,
Looked up and wished he were a bird
To whom such doubts must seem absurd.

Blessed Event

Round the three actors in any blessed event
Is always standing an invisible audience of four,
The double twins, the fallen natures of man.

On the Left they remember difficult childhoods,
On the Right they have forgotten why they were so happy,
Above sit the best decisive people,
Below they must kneel all day so as not to be governed.

Four voices just audible in the hush of any Christmas:
Accept my friendship or die.
I shall keep order and not very much will happen.
Bring me luck and of course I'll support you.
I smell blood and an era of prominent madmen.

But the Three hear nothing and are blind even to the landscape
With its towns and rivers and pretty pieces of nonsense.
He, all father, repenting their animal nights,
Cries: *Why did She have to be tortured? It is all my fault.*
Once more a virgin, She whispers: *The Future shall never suffer.*
And the New Life awkwardly touches its home, beginning to
    fumble
About in the Truth for the straight successful Way
Which will always appear to end in some dreadful defeat.

At the Grave of Henry James

The snow, less intransigeant than their marble,
Has left the defence of whiteness to these tombs,
    And all the pools at my feet
Accommodate blue now, echo such clouds as occur
To the sky, and whatever bird or mourner the passing
    Moment remarks they repeat.

While rocks, named after singular spaces
Within which images wandered once that caused
    All to tremble and offend,
Stand here in an innocent stillness, each marking the spot
Where one more series of errors lost its uniqueness
    And novelty came to an end.

To whose real advantage were such transactions,
When worlds of reflection were exchanged for trees?
    What living occasion can
Be just to the absent? Noon but reflects on itself,
And the small taciturn stone, that is the only witness
    To a great and talkative man,

Has no more judgement than my ignorant shadow
Of odious comparisons or distant clocks
    Which challenge and interfere
With the heart's instantaneous reading of time, time that is
A warm enigma no longer to you for whom I
    Surrender my private cheer,

As I stand awake on our solar fabric,
That primary machine, the earth, which gendarmes, banks
    And aspirin pre-suppose,
On which the clumsy and sad may all sit down, and any who will
Say their a-ha to the beautiful, the common locus
    Of the Master and the rose.

Shall I not especially bless you as, vexed with
My little inferior questions, I stand
    Above the bed where you rest,
Who opened such passionate arms to your *Bon* when It ran
Towards you with its overwhelming reasons pleading
    All beautifully in Its breast?

With what an innocence your hand submitted
To those formal rules that help a child to play,
    While your heart, fastidious as

A delicate nun, remained true to the rare noblesse
Of your lucid gift and, for its love, ignored the
　　Resentful muttering Mass,

Whose ruminant hatred of all that cannot
Be simplified or stolen is yet at large:
　　No death can assuage its lust
To vilify the landscape of Distinction and see
The heart of the Personal brought to a systolic standstill,
　　The Tall to diminished dust.

Preserve me, Master, from its vague incitement;
Yours be the disciplinary image that holds
　　Me back from agreeable wrong
And the clutch of eddying Muddle, lest Proportion shed
The alpine chill of her shrugging editorial shoulder
　　On my loose impromptu song.

All will be judged. Master of nuance and scruple,
Pray for me and for all writers, living or dead:
　　Because there are many whose works
Are in better taste than their lives, because there is no end
To the vanity of our calling, make intercession
　　For the treason of all clerks.

Alone

Each lover has a theory of his own
About the difference between the ache
Of being with his love, and being alone:

Why what, when dreaming, is dear flesh and bone
That really stirs the senses, when awake,
Appears a simulacrum of his own.

Narcissus disbelieves in the unknown;
He cannot join his image in the lake
So long as he assumes he is alone.

The child, the waterfall, the fire, the stone,
Are always up to mischief, though, and take
The universe for granted as their own.

The elderly, like Proust, are always prone
To think of love as a subjective fake;
The more they love, the more they feel alone.

Whatever view we hold, it must be shown
Why every lover has a wish to make
Some other kind of otherness his own:
Perhaps, in fact, we never are alone.

Leap Before You Look

The sense of danger must not disappear:
The way is certainly both short and steep,
However gradual it looks from here;
Look if you like, but you will have to leap.

Tough-minded men get mushy in their sleep
And break the by-laws any fool can keep;
It is not the convention but the fear
That has a tendency to disappear.

The worried efforts of the busy heap,
The dirt, the imprecision, and the beer
Produce a few smart wisecracks every year;
Laugh if you can, but you will have to leap.

The clothes that are considered right to wear
Will not be either sensible or cheap,
So long as we consent to live like sheep
And never mention those who disappear.

Much can be said for social savoir-faire,
But to rejoice when no one else is there
Is even harder than it is to weep;
No one is watching, but you have to leap.

A solitude ten thousand fathoms deep
Sustains the bed on which we lie, my dear:
Although I love you, you will have to leap;
Our dream of safety has to disappear.

If I Could Tell You

Time will say nothing but I told you so,
Time only knows the price we have to pay;
If I could tell you I would let you know.

If we should weep when clowns put on their show,
If we should stumble when musicians play,
Time will say nothing but I told you so.

There are no fortunes to be told, although,
Because I love you more than I can say,
If I could tell you I would let you know.

The winds must come from somewhere when they blow,
There must be reasons why the leaves decay;
Time will say nothing but I told you so.

Perhaps the roses really want to grow,
The vision seriously intends to stay;
If I could tell you I would let you know.

Suppose the lions all get up and go,
And all the brooks and soldiers run away;
Will Time say nothing but I told you so?
If I could tell you I would let you know.

Atlantis

Being set on the idea
   Of getting to Atlantis,
You have discovered of course
   Only the Ship of Fools is
Making the voyage this year,
As gales of abnormal force
   Are predicted, and that you
   Must therefore be ready to
Behave absurdly enough
   To pass for one of The Boys,
At least appearing to love
   Hard liquor, horseplay and noise.

Should storms, as may well happen,
   Drive you to anchor a week
In some old harbour-city
   Of Ionia, then speak
With her witty scholars, men
Who have proved there cannot be
   Such a place as Atlantis:
   Learn their logic, but notice
How their subtlety betrays
   A simple enormous grief;
Thus they shall teach you the ways
   To doubt that you may believe.

If, later, you run aground
   Among the headlands of Thrace
Where with torches all night long
   A naked barbaric race
Leaps frenziedly to the sound
Of conch and dissonant gong;
   On that stony savage shore
   Strip off your clothes and dance, for
Unless you are capable
   Of forgetting completely

About Atlantis, you will
   Never finish your journey.

Again, should you come to gay
   Carthage or Corinth, take part
In their endless gaiety;
   And if in some bar a tart,
As she strokes your hair, should say
'This is Atlantis, dearie,'
   Listen with attentiveness
   To her life-story: unless
You become acquainted now
   With each refuge that tries to
Counterfeit Atlantis, how
   Will you recognize the true?

Assuming you beach at last
   Near Atlantis, and begin
The terrible trek inland
   Through squalid woods and frozen
Tundras where all are soon lost;
If, forsaken then, you stand,
   Dismissal everywhere,
   Stone and snow, silence and air,
Remember the noble dead
   And honour the fate you are,
Travelling and tormented,
   Dialectic and bizarre.

Stagger onward rejoicing;
   And even then if, perhaps
Having actually got
   To the last col, you collapse
With all Atlantis gleaming
Below you yet you cannot
   Descend, you should still be proud
Just to peep at Atlantis
   In a poetic vision:
Give thanks and lie down in peace,
   Having seen your salvation.

All the little household gods
　Have started crying, but say
Good-bye now, and put to sea.
　Farewell, dear friend, farewell: may
Hermes, master of the roads
And the four dwarf Kabiri,
　Protect and serve you always;
　And may the Ancient of Days
Provide for all you must do
　His invisible guidance,
Lifting up, friend, upon you
　The light of His countenance.

In Sickness and in Health

(*For Maurice and Gwen Mandelbaum*)

Dear, all benevolence of fingering lips
That does not ask forgiveness is a noise
　At drunken feasts where Sorrow strips
To serve some glittering generalities:
Now, more than ever, we distinctly hear
The dreadful shuffle of a murderous year
And all our senses roaring as the Black
Dog leaps upon the individual back.

Whose sable genius understands too well
What code of famine can administrate
　Those inarticulate wastes where dwell
Our howling appetites: dear heart, do not
Think lightly to contrive his overthrow;
No, promise nothing, nothing, till you know
The kingdom offered by the love-lorn eyes
A land of condors, sick cattle, and dead flies.

And how contagious is its desolation,
What figures of destruction unawares
    Jump out on Love's imagination
And chase away the castles and the bears;
How warped the mirrors where our worlds are made;
What armies burn up honour, and degrade
Our will-to-order into thermal waste;
What goods are smashed that cannot be replaced.

Let no one say I Love until aware
What huge resources it will take to nurse
    One ruining speck, one tiny hair
That casts a shadow through the universe:
We are the deaf immured within a loud
And foreign language of revolt, a crowd
Of poaching hands and mouths who out of fear
Have learned a safer life than we can bear.

Nature by nature in unnature ends:
Echoing each other like two waterfalls,
    Tristan, Isolde, the great friends,
Make passion out of passion's obstacles,
Deliciously postponing their delight,
Prolong frustration till it lasts all night,
Then perish lest Brangaene's worldly cry
Should sober their cerebral ecstasy.

But, dying, conjure up their opposite,
Don Juan, so terrified of death he hears
    Each moment recommending it
And knows no argument to counter theirs:
Trapped in their vile affections, he must find
Angels to keep him chaste; a helpless, blind,
Unhappy spook, he haunts the urinals,
Existing solely by their miracles.

That syllogistic nightmare must reject
The disobedient phallus for the sword;

The lovers of themselves collect,
And Eros is politically adored:
New Machiavellis, flying through the air,
Express a metaphysical despair,
Murder their last voluptuous sensation,
All passion in one passionate negation.

Beloved, we are always in the wrong,
Handling so clumsily our stupid lives,
   Suffering too little or too long,
   Too careful even in our selfish loves:
The decorative manias we obey
Die in grimaces round us every day,
Yet through their tohu-bohu comes a voice
Which utters an absurd command — Rejoice.

Rejoice. What talent for the makeshift thought
A living corpus out of odds and ends?
   What pedagogic patience taught
Pre-occupied and savage elements
To dance into a segregated charm?
Who showed the whirlwind how to be an arm,
And gardened from the wilderness of space
The sensual properties of one dear face?

Rejoice, dear love, in Love's peremptory word;
All chance, all love, all logic, you and I,
   Exist by grace of the Absurd,
And without conscious artifice we die:
So, lest we manufacture in our flesh
The lie of our divinity afresh,
Describe round our chaotic malice now,
The arbitrary circle of a vow.

That reason may not force us to commit
That sin of the high-minded, sublimation,
   Which damns the soul by praising it,
Force our desire, O Essence of creation,

To seek Thee always in Thy substances,
Till the performance of those offices
Our bodies, Thine opaque enigmas, do,
Configure Thy transparent justice too.

Lest animal bias should decline our wish
For Thy perfection to identify
    Thee with Thy things, to worship fish,
Or solid apples, or the wavering sky,
Our intellectual motions with Thy light
To such intense vibration, Love, excite,
That we give forth a quiet none can tell
From that in which the lichens live so well.

That this round O of faithfulness we swear
May never wither to an empty nought
    Nor petrify into a square,
Mere habits of affection freeze our thought
In their inert society, lest we
Mock virtue with its pious parody
And take our love for granted, Love permit
Temptations always to endanger it.

Lest, blurring with old moonlight of romance
The landscape of our blemishes, we try
    To set up shop on Goodwin Sands,
That we, though lovers, may love soberly,
O Fate, O *Felix Osculum*, to us
Remain nocturnal and mysterious:
Preserve us from presumption and delay,
And hold us to the ordinary way.

Many Happy Returns

(For John Rettger)

Johnny, since to-day is
February the twelfth when
Neighbours and relations
    Think of you and wish,
Though a staunch Aquarian,
Graciously accept the
Verbal celebrations
    Of a doubtful Fish.

Seven years ago you
Warmed your mother's heart by
Making a successful
    Début on our stage;
Naïveté's an act that
You already know you
Cannot get away with
    Even at your age.

So I wish you first a
Sense of theatre; only
Those who love illusion
    And know it will go far:
Otherwise we spend our
Lives in a confusion
Of what we say and do with
    Who we really are.

You will any day now
Have this revelation;
'Why, we're all like people
    Acting in a play.'
And will suffer, Johnny,
Man's unique temptation
Precisely at the moment
    You utter this cliché.

Remember if you can then,
Only the All-Father
Can change the cast or give them
    Easier lines to say;
Deliberate interference
With others for their own good
Is not allowed the author
    Of the play within The Play.

Just because our pride's an
Evil there's no end to,
Birthdays and the arts are
    Justified, for when
We consciously pretend to
Own the earth or play at
Being gods, thereby we
    Own that we are men.

As a human creature
You will all too often
Forget your proper station,
    Johnny, like us all;
Therefore let your birthday
Be a wild occasion
Like a Saturnalia
    Or a Servants' Ball.

What else shall I wish you?
Following convention
Shall I wish you Beauty
    Money, Happiness?
Or anything you mention?
No, for I recall an
Ancient proverb; — Nothing
    Fails like a success.

What limping devil sets our
Head and heart at variance,
That each time the Younger
    Generation sails,

The old and weather-beaten
Deny their own experience
And pray the gods to send them
   Calm seas, auspicious gales?

I'm not such an idiot
As to claim the power
To peer into the vistas
   Of your future, still
I'm prepared to guess you
Have not found your life as
Easy as your sister's
   And you never will.

If I'm right about this,
May you in your troubles,
Neither (like so many
   In the U.S.A.)
Be ashamed of any
Suffering as vulgar,
Nor bear them like a hero
   In the biggest way.

All the possibilities
It had to reject are
What give life and warmth to
   An actual character;
The roots of wit and charm tap
Secret springs of sorrow,
Every brilliant doctor
   Hides a murderer.

Then, since all self-knowledge
Tempts man into envy,
May you, by acquiring
   Proficiency in what
Whitehead calls the art of
Negative Prehension,
Love without desiring
   All that you are not.

Tao is a tightrope,
So to keep your balance,
May you always, Johnny,
　Manage to combine
Intellectual talents
With a sensual gusto,
The Socratic Doubt with
　The Socratic Sign.

That is all that I can
Think of at this moment
And it's time I brought these
　Verses to a close:
Happy Birthday, Johnny,
Live beyond your income,
Travel for enjoyment,
　Follow your own nose.

Mundus et Infans

(For Albert and Angelyn Stevens)

Kicking his mother until she let go of his soul
Has given him a healthy appetite: clearly, her rôle
　In the New Order must be
To supply and deliver his raw materials free;
　Should there be any shortage,
She will be held responsible; she also promises
To show him all such attentions as befit his age.
　Having dictated peace,

With one fist clenched behind his head, heel drawn up to thigh
The cocky little ogre dozes off, ready,
　Though, to take on the rest
Of the world at the drop of a hat or the mildest
　Nudge of the impossible,

Resolved, cost what it may, to seize supreme power and
Sworn to resist tyranny to the death with all
    Forces at his command.

A pantheist not a solipsist, he co-operates
With a universe of large and noisy feeling-states
    Without troubling to place
Them anywhere special, for, to his eyes, Funnyface
    Or Elephant as yet
Mean nothing. His distinction between Me and Us
Is a matter of taste; his seasons are Dry and Wet;
    He thinks as his mouth does.

Still, his loud iniquity is still what only the
Greatest of saints become — someone who does not lie:
    He because he cannot
Stop the vivid present to think, they by having got
    Past reflection into
A passionate obedience in time. We have our Boy-
Meets-Girl era of mirrors and muddle to work through,
    Without rest, without joy.

Therefore we love him because his judgments are so
Frankly subjective that his abuse carries no
    Personal sting. We should
Never dare offer our helplessness as a good
    Bargain, without at least
Promising to overcome a misfortune we blame
History or Banks or the Weather for: but this beast
    Dares to exist without shame.

Let him praise our Creator with the top of his voice,
Then, and the motions of his bowels; let us rejoice
    That he lets us hope, for
He may never become a fashionable or
    Important personage:
However bad he may be, he has not yet gone mad;
Whoever we are now, we were no worse at his age;
    So of course we ought to be glad

When he bawls the house down. Has he not a perfect right
To remind us at every moment how we quite
   Rightly expect each other
To go upstairs or for a walk, if we must cry over
   Spilt milk, such as our wish
That, since apparently we shall never be above
Either or both, we had never learned to distinguish
   Between hunger and love?

Few and Simple

Whenever you are thought, the mind
Amazes me with all the kind
Old such-and-such it says about you
As if I were the one that you
Attach unique importance to,
Not one who would but didn't get you.

Startling us both at certain hours,
The flesh that mind insists is ours,
Though I, for one, by now know better,
Gets ready for no-matter-what
As if it had forgotten that
What happens is another matter.

Few as they are, these facts are all
The richest moment can recall,
However it may choose to group them,
And, simple as they look, enough
To make the most ingenious love
Think twice of trying to escape them.

The Lesson

The first time that I dreamed, we were in flight,
And fagged with running; there was civil war,
A valley full of thieves and wounded bears.

Farms blazed behind us; turning to the right,
We came at once to a tall house, its door
Wide open, waiting for its long-lost heirs.

An elderly clerk sat on the bedroom stairs
Writing; but we had tiptoed past him when
He raised his head and stuttered — 'Go away'.
We wept and begged to stay:
He wiped his pince-nez, hesitated, then
Said no, he had no power to give us leave;
Our lives were not in order; we must leave.

*   *   *

The second dream began in a May wood;
We had been laughing; your blue eyes were kind,
Your excellent nakedness without disdain.

Our lips met, wishing universal good;
But, on their impact, sudden flame and wind
Fetched you away and turned me loose again

To make a focus for a wide wild plain,
Dead level and dead silent and bone dry,
Where nothing could have suffered, sinned, or grown.
On a high chair alone
I sat, a little master, asking why
The cold and solid object in my hands
Should be a human hand, one of your hands.

*   *   *

And the last dream was this: we were to go
To a great banquet and a Victory Ball
After some tournament or dangerous test.

Our cushions were of crimson velvet, so
We must have won; though there were crowns for all,
Ours were of gold, of paper all the rest.

Fair, wise or funny was each famous guest,
Love smiled at Courage over priceless glass,
And rockets died in hundreds to express
Our learned carelessness.
A band struck up; all over the green grass
A sea of paper crowns rose up to dance:
Ours were too heavy; we did not dance.

* * *

I woke. You were not there. But as I dressed
Anxiety turned to shame, feeling all three
Intended one rebuke. For had not each
In its own way tried to teach
My will to love you that it cannot be,
As I think, of such consequence to want
What anyone is given, if they want?

A Healthy Spot

They're nice — one would never dream of going over
Any contract of theirs with a magnifying
Glass, or of locking up one's letters — also
Kind and efficient — one gets what one asks for.
Just what is wrong, then, that, living among them,
One is constantly struck by the number of
Happy marriages and unhappy people?
They attend all the lectures on Post-War Problems,
For they do mind, they honestly want to help; yet,
As they notice the earth in their morning papers,
What sense do they make of its folly and horror
Who have never, one is convinced, felt a sudden
Desire to torture the cat or do a strip-tease
In a public place? Have they ever, one wonders,

Wanted so much to see a unicorn, even
A dead one? Probably. But they won't say so,
Ignoring by tacit consent our hunger
For eternal life, that caged rebuked question
Occasionally let out at clambakes or
College reunions, and which the smoking-room story
Alone, ironically enough, stands up for.

The Model

Generally, reading palms or handwriting or faces
   Is a job of translation, since the kind
      Gentleman often is
A seducer, the frowning schoolgirl may
      Be dying to be asked to stay;
But the body of this old lady exactly indicates her mind;

Rorschach or Binet could not add to what a fool can see
   From the plain fact that she is alive and well;
      For when one is eighty
Even a teeny-weeny bit of greed
      Makes one very ill indeed,
And a touch of despair is instantaneously fatal:

Whether the town once drank bubbly out of her shoes or
      whether
   She was a governess with a good name
      In Church circles, if her
Husband spoiled her or if she lost her son,
      Is by this time all one.
She survived whatever happened; she forgave; she became.

So the painter may please himself; give her an English park,
   Rice-fields in China, or a slum tenement;
      Make the sky light or dark;
   Put green plush behind her or a red brick wall.
      She will compose them all,
Centring the eye on their essential human element.

Three Dreams

I

How still it is; our horses
Have moved into the shade, our mothers
Have followed their migrating gardens.

Curlews on kettle moraines
Foretell the end of time,
The doom of paradox.

But lovelorn sighs ascend
From wretched greedy regions
Which cannot include themselves;

And a freckled orphan flinging
Ducks and drakes at a pond,
Stops looking for stones,

And wishes he were a steamboat
Or Lugalzaggisi, the loud
Tyrant of Erech and Umma.

II

Lights are moving
On domed hills
Where little monks
Get up in the dark.

Though wild volcanoes
Growl in their sleep
At a green world,
Inside their cloisters

They sit, translating
A vision into
The vulgar lingo
Of armed cities,

Where brides arrive
Through great doors,
And robbers' bones
Dangle from gallows.

III

Bending forward
With stern faces,
Pilgrims puff
Up the steep bank
In huge hats.

Shouting, I run
In the other direction,
Cheerful, unchaste,
With open shirt
And tinkling guitar.

The Fall of Rome

(for Cyril Connolly)

The piers are pummelled by the waves;
In a lonely field the rain
Lashes an abandoned train;
Outlaws fill the mountain caves.

Fantastic grow the evening gowns;
Agents of the Fisc pursue
Absconding tax-defaulters through
The sewers of provincial towns.

Private rites of magic send
The temple prostitutes to sleep;
All the literati keep
An imaginary friend.

Cerebrotonic Cato may
Extol the Ancient Disciplines,
But the muscle-bound Marines
Mutiny for food and pay.

Caesar's double-bed is warm
As an unimportant clerk
Writes *I DO NOT LIKE MY WORK*
On a pink official form.

Unendowed with wealth or pity,
Little birds with scarlet legs,
Sitting on their speckled eggs,
Eye each flu-infected city.

Altogether elsewhere, vast
Herds of reindeer move across
Miles and miles of golden moss,
Silently and very fast.

Nursery Rhyme

Their learned kings bent down to chat with frogs;
This was until the Battle of the Bogs.
The key that opens is the key that rusts.

Their cheerful kings made toffee on their stoves;
This was until the Rotting of the Loaves.
The robins vanish when the ravens come.

That was before the coaches reached the bogs;
Now woolly bears pursue the spotted dogs.
A witch can make an ogre out of mud.

That was before the weevils ate the loaves;
Now blinded bears invade the orange groves.
A witch can make an ogre out of mud.

The woolly bears have polished off the dogs;
Our bowls of milk are full of drowning frogs.
The robins vanish when the ravens come.

The blinded bears have rooted up the groves;
Our poisoned milk boils over on our stoves.
The key that opens is the key that rusts.

In Schrafft's

Having finished the Blue-plate Special
And reached the coffee stage,
Stirring her cup she sat,
A somewhat shapeless figure
Of indeterminate age
In an undistinguished hat.

When she lifted her eyes it was plain
That our globular furore,
Our international rout
Of sin and apparatus
And dying men galore,
Was not being bothered about.

Which of the seven heavens
Was responsible her smile
Wouldn't be sure but attested
That, whoever it was, a god
Worth kneeling-to for a while
Had tabernacled and rested.

Under Which Lyre
A Reactionary Tract for the Times

(Phi Beta Kappa Poem, Harvard, 1946)

Ares at last has quit the field,
The bloodstains on the bushes yield
    To seeping showers,
And in their convalescent state
The fractured towns associate
    With summer flowers.

Encamped upon the college plain
Raw veterans already train
    As freshman forces;
Instructors with sarcastic tongue
Shepherd the battle-weary young
    Through basic courses.

Among bewildering appliances
For mastering the arts and sciences
    They stroll or run,
And nerves that steeled themselves to slaughter
Are shot to pieces by the shorter
    Poems of Donne.

Professors back from secret missions
Resume their proper eruditions,
    Though some regret it;
They liked their dictaphones a lot,
They met some big wheels, and do not
    Let you forget it.

But Zeus' inscrutable decree
Permits the will-to-disagree
    To be pandemic,
Ordains that vaudeville shall preach
And every commencement speech
    Be a polemic.

Let Ares doze, that other war
Is instantly declared once more
    'Twixt those who follow
Precocious Hermes all the way
And those who without qualms obey
    Pompous Apollo.

Brutal like all Olympic games,
Though fought with smiles and Christian names
    And less dramatic,
This dialectic strife between
The civil gods is just as mean,
    And more fanatic.

What high immortals do in mirth
Is life and death on Middle Earth;
    Their a-historic
Antipathy forever gripes
All ages and somatic types,
    The sophomoric

Who face the future's darkest hints
With giggles or with prairie squints
    As stout as Cortez,
And those who like myself turn pale
As we approach with ragged sail
    The fattening forties.

The sons of Hermes love to play,
And only do their best when they
    Are told they oughtn't;
Apollo's children never shrink
From boring jobs but have to think
    Their work important.

Related by antithesis,
A compromise between us is
    Impossible;

Respect perhaps but friendship never:
Falstaff the fool confronts forever
    The prig Prince Hal.

If he would leave the self alone,
Apollo's welcome to the throne,
    Fasces and falcons;
He loves to rule, has always done it;
The earth would soon, did Hermes run it,
    Be like the Balkans.

But jealous of our god of dreams,
His common-sense in secret schemes
    To rule the heart;
Unable to invent the lyre,
Creates with simulated fire
    Official art.

And when he occupies a college,
Truth is replaced by Useful Knowledge;
    He pays particular
Attention to Commercial Thought,
Public Relations, Hygiene, Sport,
    In his curricula.

Athletic, extrovert and crude,
For him, to work in solitude
    Is the offence,
The goal a populous Nirvana:
His shield bears this device: *Mens sana*
    Qui mal y pense.

Today his arms, we must confess,
From Right to Left have met success,
    His banners wave
From Yale to Princeton, and the news
From Broadway to the Book Reviews
    Is very grave.

His radio Homers all day long
In over-Whitmanated song
    That does not scan,
With adjectives laid end to end,
Extol the doughnut and commend
    The Common Man.

His, too, each homely lyric thing
On sport or spousal love or spring
    Or dogs or dusters,
Invented by some court-house bard
For recitation by the yard
    In filibusters.

To him ascend the prize orations
And sets of fugal variations
    On some folk-ballad,
While dietitians sacrifice
A glass of prune-juice or a nice
    Marsh-mallow salad.

Charged with his compound of sensational
Sex plus some undenominational
    Religious matter,
Enormous novels by co-eds
Rain down on our defenceless heads
    Till our teeth chatter.

In fake Hermetic uniforms
Behind our battle-line, in swarms
    That keep alighting,
His existentialists declare
That they are in complete despair,
    Yet go on writing.

No matter; He shall be defied;
White Aphrodite is on our side:
    What though his threat

To organize us grow more critical?
Zeus willing, we, the unpolitical,
　　Shall beat him yet.

Lone scholars, sniping from the walls
Of learned periodicals,
　　Our facts defend,
Our intellectual marines,
Landing in little magazines
　　Capture a trend.

By night our student Underground
At cocktail parties whisper round
　　From ear to ear;
Fat figures in the public eye
Collapse next morning, ambushed by
　　Some witty sneer.

In our morale must lie our strength:
So, that we may behold at length
　　Routed Apollo's
Battalions melt away like fog,
Keep well the Hermetic Decalogue,
　　Which runs as follows: —

Thou shalt not do as the dean pleases,
Thou shalt not write thy doctor's thesis
　　On education,
Thou shalt not worship projects nor
Shalt thou or thine bow down before
　　Administration.

Thou shalt not answer questionnaires
Or quizzes upon World-Affairs,
　　Nor with compliance
Take any test. Thou shalt not sit
With statisticians nor commit
　　A social science.

Thou shalt not be on friendly terms
With guys in advertising firms,
        Nor speak with such
As read the Bible for its prose,
Nor, above all, make love to those
        Who wash too much.

Thou shalt not live within thy means
Nor on plain water and raw greens.
        If thou must choose
Between the chances, choose the odd;
Read *The New Yorker*, trust in God;
        And take short views.

Music Is International

(*Phi Beta Kappa Poem, Columbia, 1947*)

Orchestras have so long been speaking
This universal language that the Greek
        And the Barbarian have both mastered
Its enigmatic grammar which at last
        Says all things well. But who is worthy?
What is sweet? What is sound? Much of the earth
        Is austere, her temperate regions
Swarming with cops and robbers; germs besiege
        The walled towns and among the living
The captured outnumber the fugitive.
        Where silence is coldest and darkest,
Among those staring blemishes that mark
        War's havocking slot, it is easy
To guess what dreams such vaulting cries release:
        The unamerican survivor
Hears angels drinking fruit-juice with their wives
        Or making money in an open
Unpolicied air. But what is our hope,
        As with an ostentatious rightness

226

These gratuitous sounds like water and light
   Bless the Republic? Do they sponsor
In us the mornes and motted mammelons,
   The sharp streams and sottering springs of
A commuter's wish, where each frescade rings
   With melodious booing and hooing
As some elegant lovejoy deigns to woo
   And nothing dreadful ever happened?
Probably yes. We are easy to trap,
   Being Adam's children, as thirsty
For mere illusion still as when the first
   Comfortable heresy crooned to
The proud flesh founded on the self-made wound,
   And what we find rousing or touching
Tells us little and confuses us much.
   As Shaw said — Music is the brandy
Of the damned. It was from the good old grand
   Composers the progressive kind of
Tyrant learned how to melt the legal mind
   With a visceral A-ha; fill a
Dwarf's ears with sforzandos and the dwarf will
   Believe he's a giant; the orchestral
Metaphor bamboozles the most oppressed
   — As a trombone the clerk will bravely
Go oompah-oompah to his minor grave —,
   So that today one recognises
The Machiavel by the hair in his eyes,
   His conductor's hands. Yet the jussive
Elohim are here too, asking for us
   Through the noise. To forgive is not so
Simple as it is made to sound; a lot
   Of time will be quite wasted, many
Promising days end badly, and again
   We shall offend: but let us listen
To the song which seems to absorb all this,
   For these halcyon structures are useful
As structures go — though not to be confused
   With anything really important
Like feeding strays or looking pleased when caught

By a bore or a hideola;
Deserving nothing, the sensible soul
    Will rejoice at the sudden mansion
Of any joy; besides, there is a chance
    We may some day need very much to
Remember when we were happy — one such
    Future would be the exile's ending
With no graves to visit, no socks to mend,
    Another to be short of breath yet
Staying on to oblige, postponing death —
    Listen! Even the dinner waltz in
Its formal way is a voice that assaults
    International wrong, so quickly,
Completely delivering to the sick,
    Sad, soiled prosopon of our ageing
Present the perdition of all her rage.

The Duet

    All winter long the huge sad lady
Sang to her warm house of the heart betrayed:
    Love lies delirious and a-dying,
The purlieus are shaken by his wild cry.
    But back across the fret dividing
His wildernesses from her floral side,
    All winter long a scrunty beggar
With one glass eye and one hickory leg,
    Stumping about half-drunk through stony
Ravines and over dead volcanic cones,
    Refused her tragic hurt, declaring
A happy passion to the freezing air,
    Turning his barrel-organ, playing
Lanterloo, my lovely, my First-of-May.

    Louder on nights when in cold glory
The full moon made its meditative tour,

To rich chords from her grand black piano
She sang the disappointment that is Man
   For all her lawns and orchards: *Slowly*
The spreading ache bechills the rampant glow
   Of fortune-hunting blood, time conjures
The moskered ancestral tower to plunge
   From its fastidious cornice down to
The pigsties far below, the oaks turn brown,
   The cute little botts of the sailors
Are snapped up by the sea. But to her gale
   Of sorrow from the moonstruck darkness
That ragged runagate opposed his spark,
   For still his scrannel music-making
In tipsy joy across the gliddered lake,
   Praising for all those rocks and craters
The green refreshments of the watered state,
   Cried Nonsense to her large repining:
The windows have opened, a royal wine
   Is poured out for the subtle pudding;
Light Industry is humming in the wood
   And blue birds bless us from the fences:
We know the time and where to find our friends.

Pleasure Island

What there is as a surround to our figures
   Is very old, very big,
Very formidable indeed; the ocean
   Stares right past us as though
No one here was worth drowning, and the eye, true
   Blue all summer, of the sky
Would not miss a huddle of huts related
   By planks, a dock, a state
Of undress and improvised abandon
   Upon unshadowed sand.
To send a cry of protest or a call for
   Protection up into all

229

Those dazzling miles, to add, however sincerely,
    One's occasional tear
To that volume, would be rather silly,
    Nor is there one small hill
For the hopeful to climb, one tree for the hopeless
    To sit under and mope;
The coast is a blur and without meaning
    The churches and routines
Which stopped there and never cared or dared to
    Cross over to interfere
With this outpost where nothing is wicked
    But to be sorry or sick,
But one thing unneighbourly, work. Sometimes
    A visitor may come
With notebooks intending to make its quiet
    Emptiness his ally
In accomplishing immortal chapters,
    But the hasty tap-tap-tap
Of his first day becomes by the second
    A sharp spasmodic peck
And by the third is extinct; we find him
    Next improving his mind
On the beach with a book, but the dozing
    Afternoon is opposed
To rhyme and reason and chamber music,
    The plain sun has no use
For the printing press, the wheel, the electric
    Light, and the waves reject
Sympathy: soon he gives in, stops stopping
    To think, lets his book drop
And lies, like us, on his stomach watching
    As bosom, backside, crotch
Or other sacred trophy is borne in triumph
    Past his adoring by
Souls he does not try to like; then, getting
    Up, gives all to the wet
Clasps of the sea or surrenders his scruples
    To some great gross braying group
That will be drunk till Fall. The tide rises

And falls, our household ice
Drips to death in the dark and our friendships
   Prepare for a weekend
They will probably not survive: for our
   Lenient amusing shore
Knows in fact about all the dyings, is in
   Fact our place, namely this
Place of a skull, a place where the rose of
   Self-punishment will grow.
The sunset happens, the bar is copious
   With fervent life that hopes
To make sense, but down the beach some decaying
   Spirit shambles away,
Kicking idly at driftwood and dead shellfish
   And excusing itself
To itself with evangelical gestures
   For having failed the test:
The moon is up there, but without warning,
   A little before dawn,
Miss Lovely, life and soul of the party,
   Wakes with a dreadful start,
Sure that whatever — O God! — she is in for
   Is about to begin,
Or hearing, beyond the hushabye noises
   Of sea and Me, just a voice
Ask, as one might the time or a trifle
   Extra, her money and her life.

A Walk After Dark

A cloudless night like this
Can set the spirit soaring:
After a tiring day
The clockwork spectacle is
Impressive in a slightly boring
Eighteenth-century way.

It soothed adolescence a lot
To meet so shameless a stare;
The things I did could not
Be so shocking as they said
If that would still be there
After the shocked were dead.

Now, unready to die
But already at the stage
When one starts to dislike the young,
I am glad those points in the sky
May also be counted among
The creatures of middle-age.

It's cosier thinking of night
As more an Old People's Home
Than a shed for a faultless machine,
That the red pre-Cambrian light
Is gone like Imperial Rome
Or myself at seventeen.

Yet however much we may like
The stoic manner in which
The classical authors wrote,
Only the young and the rich
Have the nerve or the figure to strike
The lacrimae rerum note.

For the present stalks abroad
Like the past and its wronged again
Whimper and are ignored,
And the truth cannot be hid;
Somebody chose their pain,
What needn't have happened did.

Occurring this very night
By no established rule,
Some event may already have hurled

Its first little No at the right
Of the laws we accept to school
Our post-diluvian world:

But the stars burn on overhead,
Unconscious of final ends,
As I walk home to bed,
Asking what judgment waits
My person, all my friends,
And these United States.

Part IV

1948-1957

In Transit

Let out where two fears intersect, a point selected
    Jointly by general staffs and engineers,
In a wet land, facing rough oceans, never invaded
    By Caesars or a cartesian doubt, I stand,
Pale, half asleep, inhaling its new fresh air that smells
    So strongly of soil and grass, of toil and gender,
But not for long: a professional friend is at hand
    Who smiling leads us indoors; we follow in file,

Obeying that fond peremptory tone reserved for those
    Nervously sick and children one cannot trust,
Who might be tempted by ponds or learn some disgusting
    Trick from a ragamuffin. Through modern panes
I admire a limestone hill I have no permission to climb
    And the pearly clouds of a sunset that seems
Oddly early to me: maybe an ambitious lad stares back,
    Dreaming of elsewhere and our godlike freedom.

Somewhere are places where we have really been, dear spaces
    Of our deeds and faces, scenes we remember
As unchanging because there we changed, where shops have
        names,
    Dogs bark in the dark at a stranger's footfall
And crops grow ripe and cattle fatten under the kind
    Protection of a godling or goddessling
Whose affection has been assigned them, to heed their needs and
    Plead in heaven the special case of their place.

Somewhere, too, unique for each, his frontier dividing
    Past from future, reached and crossed without warning:
That bridge where an ageing destroyer takes his last salute,
    In his rear all rivals fawning, in cages
Or dead, ahead a field of wrath; and that narrow pass where,
    Late from a sullen childhood, a fresh creator
Yields, glowing, to a boyish rapture, wild gothic peaks above him,
    Below, Italian sunshine, Italian flesh.

But here we are nowhere, unrelated to day or to Mother
    Earth in love or in hate; our occupation
Leaves no trace on this place or each other who do not
    Meet in its mere enclosure but are exposed
As objects for speculation, aggressive creatures
    On their way to their prey but now quite docile,
Told to wait and controlled by a voice that from time to time calls
    Some class of souls to foregather at the gate.

It calls me again to our plane and soon we are floating above
    A possessed congested surface, a world: down there
Motives and natural processes are stirred by spring
    And wrongs and graves grow greenly; slaves in quarries
Against their wills feel the will to live renewed by the song
    Of a loose bird, maculate cities are spared
Through the prayers of illiterate saints, and an ancient
    Feud re-opens with the debacle of a river.

In Praise of Limestone

If it form the one landscape that we, the inconstant ones,
    Are consistently homesick for, this is chiefly
Because it dissolves in water. Mark these rounded slopes
    With their surface fragrance of thyme and, beneath,
A secret system of caves and conduits; hear the springs
    That spurt out everywhere with a chuckle,
Each filling a private pool for its fish and carving
    Its own little ravine whose cliffs entertain

238

The butterfly and the lizard; examine this region
    Of short distances and definite places:
What could be more like Mother or a fitter background
    For her son, the flirtatious male who lounges
Against a rock in the sunlight, never doubting
    That for all his faults he is loved; whose works are but
Extensions of his power to charm? From weathered outcrop
    To hill-top temple, from appearing waters to
Conspicuous fountains, from a wild to a formal vineyard,
    Are ingenious but short steps that a child's wish
To receive more attention than his brothers, whether
    By pleasing or teasing, can easily take.

Watch, then, the band of rivals as they climb up and down
    Their steep stone gennels in twos and threes, at times
Arm in arm, but never, thank God, in step; or engaged
    On the shady side of a square at midday in
Voluble discourse, knowing each other too well to think
    There are any important secrets, unable
To conceive a god whose temper-tantrums are moral
    And not to be pacified by a clever line
Or a good lay: for, accustomed to a stone that responds,
    They have never had to veil their faces in awe
Of a crater whose blazing fury could not be fixed;
    Adjusted to the local needs of valleys
Where everything can be touched or reached by walking,
    Their eyes have never looked into infinite space
Through the lattice-work of a nomad's comb; born lucky,
    Their legs have never encountered the fungi
And insects of the jungle, the monstrous forms and lives
    With which we have nothing, we like to hope, in common.
So, when one of them goes to the bad, the way his mind works
    Remains comprehensible: to become a pimp
Or deal in fake jewellery or ruin a fine tenor voice
    For effects that bring down the house, could happen to all
But the best and the worst of us . . .
                                    That is why, I suppose,
    The best and worst never stayed here long but sought
Immoderate soils where the beauty was not so external,

The light less public and the meaning of life
Something more than a mad camp. 'Come!' cried the granite
      wastes,
   'How evasive is your humour, how accidental
Your kindest kiss, how permanent is death.' (Saints-to-be
      Slipped away sighing.) 'Come!' purred the clays and gravels.
'On our plains there is room for armies to drill; rivers
      Wait to be tamed and slaves to construct you a tomb
In the grand manner: soft as the earth is mankind and both
      Need to be altered.' (Intendant Caesars rose and
Left, slamming the door.) But the really reckless were fetched
      By an older colder voice, the oceanic whisper:
'I am the solitude that asks and promises nothing;
      That is how I shall set you free. There is no love;
There are only the various envies, all of them sad.'
      They were right, my dear, all those voices were right
And still are; this land is not the sweet home that it looks,
      Nor its peace the historical calm of a site
Where something was settled once and for all: A backward
      And dilapidated province, connected
To the big busy world by a tunnel, with a certain
      Seedy appeal, is that all it is now? Not quite:
It has a worldly duty which in spite of itself
      It does not neglect, but calls into question
All the Great Powers assume; it disturbs our rights. The poet,
      Admired for his earnest habit of calling
The sun the sun, his mind Puzzle, is made uneasy
      By these marble statues which so obviously doubt
His antimythological myth; and these gamins,
      Pursuing the scientist down the tiled colonnade
With such lively offers, rebuke his concern for Nature's
      Remotest aspects: I, too, am reproached, for what
And how much you know. Not to lose time, not to get caught,
      Not to be left behind, not, please! to resemble
The beasts who repeat themselves, or a thing like water
      Or stone whose conduct can be predicted, these
Are our Common Prayer, whose greatest comfort is music
      Which can be made anywhere, is invisible,
And does not smell. In so far as we have to look forward

To death as a fact, no doubt we are right: But if
Sins can be forgiven, if bodies rise from the dead,
    These modifications of matter into
Innocent athletes and gesticulating fountains,
    Made solely for pleasure, make a further point:
The blessed will not care what angle they are regarded from,
    Having nothing to hide. Dear, I know nothing of
Either, but when I try to imagine a faultless love
    Or the life to come, what I hear is the murmur
Of underground streams, what I see is a limestone landscape.

Ischia

(*for Brian Howard*)

There is a time to admit how much the sword decides,
with flourishing horns to salute the conqueror,
        impassive, cloaked and great on
    horseback under his faffling flag.

Changes of heart should also occasion song, like his
who, turning back from the crusaders' harbour, broke
        with our aggressive habit
    once and for all and was the first

to see all penniless creatures as our siblings. Then
at all times it is good to praise the shining earth,
        dear to us whether we choose our
    duty or do something horrible.

Dearest to each his birthplace; but to recall a green
valley where mushrooms fatten in the summer nights
        and silvered willows copy
    the circumflexions of the stream

is not my gladness today: I am presently moved
by sun-drenched Parthenopea, my thanks are for you,
     Ischia, to whom a fair wind has
   brought me rejoicing with dear friends

from soiled productive cities. How well you correct
our injured eyes, how gently you train us to see
     things and men in perspective
   underneath your uniform light.

Noble are the plans of the shirt-sleeved engineer,
but luck, you say, does more. What design could have washed
     with such delicate yellows
   and pinks and greens your fishing ports

that lean against ample Epomeo, holding on
to the rigid folds of her skirts? The boiling springs
     which betray her secret fever,
   make limber the gout-stiffened joint

and improve the venereal act; your ambient peace
in any case is a cure for, ceasing to think
     of a way to get on, we
   learn to simply wander about

by twisting paths which at any moment reveal
some vista as an absolute goal; eastward, perhaps,
     suddenly there, Vesuvius,
   looming across the bright bland bay

like a massive family pudding, or, around
a southern point, sheer-sided Capri who by herself
     defends the cult of Pleasure,
   a jealous, sometimes a cruel, god.

Always with some cool space or shaded surface, too,
you offer a reason to sit down; tasting what bees
     from the blossoming chestnut
   or short but shapely dark-haired men

from the aragonian grape distil, your amber wine,
your coffee-coloured honey, we believe that our
            lives are as welcome to us as
        loud explosions are to your saints.

Not that you lie about pain or pretend that a time
of darkness and outcry will not come back; upon
            your quays, reminding the happy
        stranger that all is never well,

sometimes a donkey breaks out into a choking wail
of utter protest at what is the case or his
            master sighs for a Brooklyn
        where shirts are silk and pants are new,

far from tall Restituta's all-too-watchful eye,
whose annual patronage, they say, is bought with blood.
            That, blessed and formidable
        Lady, we hope is not true; but, since

nothing is free, whatever you charge shall be paid,
that these days of exotic splendour may stand out
            in each lifetime like marble
        mileposts in an alluvial land.

Under Sirius

Yes, these are the dog-days, Fortunatus:
        The heather lies limp and dead
    On the mountain, the baltering torrent
        Shrunk to a soodling thread;
Rusty the spears of the legion, unshaven its captain,
        Vacant the scholar's brain
        Under his great hat,
    Drug though She may, the Sybil utters
        A gush of table-chat.

And you yourself with a head-cold and upset stomach,
    Lying in bed till noon,
  Your bills unpaid, your much advertised
    Epic not yet begun,
Are a sufferer too. All day, you tell us, you wish
    Some earthquake would astonish,
    Or the wind of the Comforter's wing
  Unlock the prisons and translate
    The slipshod gathering.

And last night, you say, you dreamed of that bright blue morning,
    The hawthorn hedges in bloom,
  When, serene in their ivory vessels,
    The three wise Maries come,
Sossing through seamless waters, piloted in
    By sea-horse and fluent dolphin:
    Ah! how the cannons roar,
  How jocular the bells as They
    Indulge the peccant shore.

It is natural to hope and pious, of course, to believe
    That all in the end shall be well,
  But first of all, remember,
    So the Sacred Books foretell,
The rotten fruit shall be shaken. Would your hope make sense
    If today were that moment of silence,
    Before it break and drown,
  When the insurrected eagre hangs
    Over the sleeping town?

How will you look and what will you do when the basalt
    Tombs of the sorcerers shatter
  And their guardian megalopods
    Come after you pitter-patter?
How will you answer when from their qualming spring
    The immortal nymphs fly shrieking,
    And out of the open sky
  The pantocratic riddle breaks —
    'Who are you and why?'

For when in a carol under the apple-trees
    The reborn featly dance,
  There will also, Fortunatus,
    Be those who refused their chance,
Now pottering shades, querulous beside the salt-pits,
    And mawkish in their wits,
    To whom these dull dog-days
  Between event seem crowned with olive
    And golden with self-praise.

Cattivo Tempo

Sirocco brings the minor devils:
A slamming of doors
At four in the morning
Announces they are back,
Grown insolent and fat
On cheesy literature
And corny dramas,
Nibbar, demon
Of ga-ga and bêtise,
Tubervillus, demon
Of gossip and spite.

Nibbar to the writing-room
Plausibly to whisper
The nearly fine,
The almost true;
Beware of him, poet,
Lest, reading over
Your shoulder, he find
What makes him glad,
The manner arch,
The meaning blurred,
The poem bad.

Tubervillus to the dining-room
Intently to listen,
Waiting his cue;
Beware of him, friends,
Lest the talk at his prompting
Take the wrong turning,
The unbated tongue
In mischief blurt
The half-home-truth,
The fun turn ugly,
The jokes hurt.

Do not underrate them; merely
To tear up the poem
To shut the mouth
Will defeat neither:
To have got you alone
Self-confined to your bedroom
Manufacturing there
From lewdness or self-care
Some whining unmanaged
Imp of your own,
That too is their triumph.

The proper riposte is to bore them;
To scurry the dull pen
Through dull correspondence,
To wag the sharp tongue
In pigeon Italian,
Asking the socialist
Barber to guess
Or the monarchist fisherman to tell
When the wind will change,
Outwitting hell
With human obviousness.

Hunting Season

A shot: from crag to crag
    The tell-tale echoes trundle;
Some feathered he-or-she
    Is now a lifeless bundle
And, proud into a kitchen, some
Example of our tribe will come.

Down in the startled valley
    Two lovers break apart:
He hears the roaring oven
    Of a witch's heart;
Behind his murmurs of her name
She sees a marksman taking aim.

Reminded of the hour
    And that his chair is hard,
A deathless verse half done,
    One interrupted bard
Postpones his dying with a dish
Of several suffocated fish.

Fleet Visit

The sailors come ashore
Out of their hollow ships,
Mild-looking middle class boys
Who read the comic strips;
One baseball game is more
To them than fifty Troys.

They look a bit lost, set down
In this unamerican place
Where natives pass with laws
And futures of their own;
They are not here because
But only just-in-case.

The whore and ne'er-do-well
Who pester them with junk
In their grubby ways at least
Are serving the Social Beast;
They neither make nor sell —
No wonder they get drunk.

But their ships on the vehement blue
Of this harbour actually gain
From having nothing to do;
Without a human will
To tell them whom to kill
Their structures are humane

And, far from looking lost,
Look as if they were meant
To be pure abstract design
By some master of pattern and line,
Certainly worth every cent
Of the billions they must have cost.

An Island Cemetery

This graveyard with its umbrella pines
Is inferior in status to the vines
And, though new guests keep crowding in,
Must stay the size it's always been.

Where men are many, acres few,
The dead must be cultivated too,
Like seeds in any farmer's field
Are planted for the bones they yield.

It takes about eighteen months for one
To ripen into a skeleton,
To be washed, folded, packed in a small
Niche hollowed out of the cemetery wall.

Curiosity made me stop
While sextons were digging up a crop:
Bards have taken it too amiss
That Alexanders come to this.

Wherever our personalities go
(And, to tell the truth, we do not know),
The solid structures they leave behind
Are no discredit to our kind.

Mourners may miss, and they do, a face,
But at least they cannot detect a trace
Of those fish-like hungers, mammalian heats,
That kin our flesh to the coarser meats.

And who would be ashamed to own
To a patience that we share with stone,
This underlying thing in us
Which never at any time made a fuss?

Considering what our motives are,
We ought to thank our lucky star
That Love must ride to reach his ends
A mount which has no need of friends.

Not in Baedeker

There were lead-mines here before the Romans
(Is there a once that is not already?),
Then mines made the manor a looming name
In bridal portions and disputed wills
(Once it changed owners during a card-game),
Then with the coming of the steam-engine
Their heyday arrived (An Early Victorian
Traveller has left us a description:
The removal of the ore, he writes, bless him,
*Leaves a horrid gulph. The wild scene is worthy
Of the pencil of Salvator Rosa.*

The eye is awe-struck at the extraordinary
Richness of the deposits and the vast
Scale of the operations.), and then, then on
A certain day (whether of time or of rock
A lot is only so much and what ends
Ends at a definite moment) there came
Their last day, the day of the last lump, the actual
Day, now vaguely years, say sixty, ago,
When engines and all stopped. Today it would take
A geologist's look to guess that these hills
Provided roofs for some great cathedrals
(One irrevocably damaged by bombs)
And waterproof linings for the coffins
Of statesmen and actresses (all replaced),
Nor could one possibly (because of the odd
Breeding-habits of money, its even
Odder nomadic mania) discover
Where and whom the more than one large fortune
Made here has got to now. A certain place
Has gone back to being (what most of the earth is
Most of the time) in the country somewhere.

Man still however (to discourage any
Romantic glooming over the Universe
Or any one marriage of work and love)
Exists on these uplands and the present
Is not uncheerful: so-so sheep are raised
And sphagnum moss (in the Latin countries
Still used in the treatment of gunshot wounds)
Collected; even the past is not dead
But revives annually on the festival
(Which occurs in the month of the willow)
Of St. Cobalt whose saturnine image,
Crude but certainly medieval is borne
In gay procession around the parish,
Halting at each of the now filled-in shafts
To the shrill chants of little girls in white
And the sneers of the local bus-driver
(Who greases his hair and dreams of halting

For a mysterious well-dressed passenger
Who offers at once to take him to the States).
Indeed, in its own quiet way, the place can strike
Most if not all of the historical notes
Even (what place can not?) the accidental:
One September Thursday two English cyclists
Stopped here for a *fine* and afterwards strolled
Along the no longer polluted stream
As far as the Shot Tower (indirectly
Responsible in its day for the deaths
Of goodness knows how many grouse, wild duck
And magnificent stags) where the younger
(Whose promise one might have guessed even then
Would come to nothing), using a rotting
Rickety gallery for a lectern,
To amuse his friend gave an imitation
Of a clergyman with a cleft palate.

Ode to Gaea

From this new culture of the air we finally see,
far-shining in excellence, what our Mother, the
            nicest daughter of Chaos, would
        admire could she look in a glass,

and what, in her eyes, is natural: it is the old
grand style of gesture we watch as, heavy with cold,
            the top-waters of all her
        northern seas take their vernal plunge,

and suddenly her desolations, salt as blood,
prolix yet terse, are glamorously carpeted
            with great swatches of plankton,
        delicious spreads of nourishment,

while, in her realm of solids, lively dots expand,
companionship becomes an unstaid passion and
            leaves by the mile hide tons of
        pied pebbles that will soon be birds.

Now that we know how she looks, she seems more mysterious
than when, in her *partibus infidelibus*,
            we painted sizzling dragons
        and wizards reading upside down,

but less approachable: where she joins girl's-ear lakes
to bird's-foot deltas with lead-blue squiggles she makes,
            surely, a value judgment,
        'of pure things Water is the best,'

but how does she rank wheelwrights? One doubts if she knows
which sub-species of folly is peculiar to those
            pretty molehills, where on that
        pocket-handkerchief of a plain

the syntax changes: peering down sleepily at
a crenellated shore, the tired old diplomat
            becomes embarrassed — Should he
        smile for 'our great good ally', scowl

at 'that vast and detestable empire' or choose
the sneer reserved for certain Southern countries 'whose
            status and moral climate
        we have no desire, sir, to emulate'?

But why we should feel neglected on mountain drives,
unpopular in woods, is quite clear; the older lives
            have no wish to be stood in
        rows or at right angles: below,

straight as its railroads, cutting diagonally across
a positivist republic, two lines of moss
            show where the Devil's Causeway
        drew pilgrims thirteen gods ago,

and on this eve of whispers and tapped telephones
before the Ninth Catastrophe, square corner-stones
        still distinguish a fortress
    of the High Kings from untutored rock.

Tempting to mortals is the fancy of half-concerned
Gods in the sky, of a bored Thunderer who turned
        from the Troy-centred grief to
    watch the Hippemolgoi drink their milk,

and how plausible from his look-point: we may well
shake a weak fist one day at this vision, but the spell
        of high places will haunt us
    long after our jaunt has declined,

as soon it must, to the hard ground. Where six foot is tall,
good-manners will ask easy riddles like 'Why are all
        the rowdiest marches and the
    most venomous iambics composed

by lame clergymen?', will tell no tales which end in worse
disaster than that of the tipsy poet who cursed
        a baby for whom later
    he came to sigh. So we were taught

before the Greater Engines came and the police
who go with them, when the long rivers ran through peace
        and the holy laws of Speech were
    held in awe, even by evil tongues,

and manners, maybe, will stand us in better stead,
down there, than a kantian conscience. From overhead
        much harm is discernible,
    farms unroofed and harbour-works wrecked

in the Second Assault; frank to an ungrieving sky
as still they look, too many fertilities lie
        in dread of the tormentor's
    fondling finger, and in the few

that still have poky shops and audiences of one,
many are overweight, the pious peasant's only son,
   goading their crumpled faces
  down innocence-corrupting roads,

dreams of cities where his cows are whores. When the wise
wilt in the glare of the Shadow, the stern advise
   tribute, and the large-hearted
  already talk Its gibberish,

perhaps a last stand in the passes will be made
by those whose Valhalla would be hearing verse by Praed
   or arias by Rossini
  between two entrées by Carême.

We hope so. But who on Cupid's Coming would care to bet?
More than one World's Bane has been scotched before this, yet
   Justice during his *Te Deum*
  slipped away sighing from the hero's pew,

and Earth, till the end, will be Herself. She has never been moved
except by Amphion, and orators have not improved
   since misled Athens perished
  upon Sicilian marble: what,

to Her, the real one, can our good landscapes be but lies,
those woods where tigers chum with deer and no root dies,
   that tideless bay where children
  play Bishop on a golden shore?

Bucolics

1. WINDS

(For Alexis Leger)

Deep, deep below our violences,
Quite still, lie our First Dad, his watch
  And many little maids,
But the boneless winds that blow
  Round law-court and temple
Recall to Metropolis
  That Pliocene Friday when,
At His holy insufflation
  (Had He picked a teleost
Or an arthropod to inspire,
  Would our death also have come?)
One bubble-brained creature said; —
  'I am loved, therefore I am' —:
And well by now might the lion
  Be lying down with the kid,
Had he stuck to that logic.

Winds make weather; weather
Is what nasty people are
  Nasty about and the nice
Show a common joy in observing:
  When I seek an image
For our Authentic City,
  (Across what brigs of dread,
Down what gloomy galleries,
  Must we stagger or crawl
Before we may cry — O look !?)
  I see old men in hall-ways
Tapping their barometers,
  Or a lawn over which
The first thing after breakfast,
  A paterfamilias
Hurries to inspect his rain-gauge.

Goddess of winds and wisdom,
    When, on some windless day
Of dejection, unable
    To name or to structure,
Your poet with bodily tics,
    Scratching, tapping his teeth,
Tugging the lobe of an ear,
    Unconsciously invokes You,
Show Your good nature, allow
    Rooster or whistling maid
To fetch him Arthur O'Bower;
    Then, if moon-faced Nonsense,
That erudite forger, stalk
    Through the seven kingdoms,
Set Your poplars a-shiver
    To warn Your clerk lest he
Die like an Old Believer
    For some spurious reading:
And in all winds, no matter
    Which of Your twelve he may hear,
Equinox gales at midnight
    Howling through marram grass,
Or a faint susurration
    Of pines on a cloudless
Afternoon in midsummer,
    Let him feel You present,
That every verbal rite
    May be fittingly done,
And done in anamnesis
    Of what is excellent
Yet a visible creature,
    Earth, Sky, a few dear names.

2. WOODS

(For Nicholas Nabakov)

Sylvan meant savage in those primal woods
Piero di Cosimo so loved to draw,
Where nudes, bears, lions, sows with women's heads,
Mounted and murdered and ate each other raw,
Nor thought the lightning-kindled bush to tame
But, flabbergasted, fled the useful flame.

Reduced to patches, owned by hunting squires,
Of villages with ovens and a stocks,
They whispered still of most unsocial fires,
Though Crown and Mitre warned their silly flocks
The pasture's humdrum rhythms to approve
And to abhor the licence of the grove.

Guilty intention still looks for a hotel
That wants no details and surrenders none;
A wood is that, and throws in charm as well,
And many a semi-innocent, undone,
Has blamed its nightingales who round the deed
Sang with such sweetness of a happy greed.

Those birds, of course, did nothing of the sort,
And, as for sylvan nature, if you take
A snapshot at a picnic, O how short
And lower-ordersy the Gang will look
By those vast lives that never took another
And are not scared of gods, ghosts, or stepmother.

Among these coffins of its by-and-by
The Public can (it cannot on a coast)
Bridle its skirt-and-bargain-chasing eye,
And where should an austere philologist
Relax but in the very world of shade
From which the matter of his field was made.

Old sounds re-educate an ear grown coarse,
As Pan's green father suddenly raps out
A burst of undecipherable Morse,
And cuckoos mock in Welsh, and doves create
In rustic English over all they do
To rear their modern family of two.

Now here, now there, some loosened element,
A fruit in vigour or a dying leaf,
Utters its private idiom for descent,
And late man, listening through his latter grief,
Hears, close or far, the oldest of his joys,
Exactly as it was, the water noise.

A well-kempt forest begs Our Lady's grace;
Someone is not disgusted, or at least
Is laying bets upon the human race
Retaining enough decency to last;
The trees encountered on a country stroll
Reveal a lot about a country's soul.

A small grove massacred to the last ash,
An oak with heart-rot, give away the show:
This great society is going smash;
They cannot fool us with how fast they go,
How much they cost each other and the gods.
A culture is no better than its woods.

3. MOUNTAINS

(For Hedwig Petzold)

I know a retired dentist who only paints mountains,
    But the Masters rarely care
That much, who sketch them in beyond a holy face
    Or a highly dangerous chair;
While a normal eye perceives them as a wall
Between worse and better, like a child, scolded in France,

Who wishes he were crying on the Italian side of the Alps:
    Caesar does not rejoice when high ground
        Makes a darker map,
    Nor does Madam. Why should they? A serious being
        Cries out for a gap.

And it is curious how often in steep places
    You meet someone short who frowns,
A type you catch beheading daisies with a stick:
    Small crooks flourish in big towns,
But perfect monsters — remember Dracula —
Are bred on crags in castles. Those unsmiling parties,
Clumping off at dawn in the gear of their mystery
    For points up, are a bit alarming;
        They have the balance, nerve,
And habit of the Spiritual, but what God
        Does their Order serve?

A civil man is a citizen. Am I
    To see in the Lake District, then,
Another bourgeois invention like the piano?
    Well, I won't. How can I, when
I wish I stood now on a platform at Penrith,
Zurich, or any junction at which you leave the express
For a local that swerves off soon into a cutting? Soon
    Tunnels begin, red farms disappear,
        Hedges turn to walls,
Cows become sheep, you smell peat or pinewood, you hear
        Your first waterfalls,

And what looked like a wall turns out to be a world
    With measurements of its own
And a style of gossip. To manage the Flesh,
    When angels of ice and stone
Stand over her day and night who make it so plain
They detest any kind of growth, does not encourage
Euphemisms for the effort: here wayside crucifixes
    Bear witness to a physical outrage,
        And serenades too

Stick to bare fact; 'O my girl has a goitre,
  I've a hole in my shoe!'

Dour. Still, a fine refuge. That boy behind his goats
  Has the round skull of a clan
That fled with bronze before a tougher metal,
  And that quiet old gentleman
With a cheap room at the Black Eagle used to own
Three papers but is not received in Society now:
These farms can always see a panting government coming;
  I'm nordic myself, but even so
    I'd much rather stay
Where the nearest person who could have me hung is
    Some ridges away.

To be sitting in privacy, like a cat
  On the warm roof of a loft,
Where the high-spirited son of some gloomy tarn
  Comes sprinting down through a green croft,
Bright with flowers laid out in exquisite splodges
Like a Chinese poem, while, near enough, a real darling
Is cooking a delicious lunch, would keep me happy for
  What? Five minutes? For an uncatlike
    Creature who has gone wrong,
Five minutes on even the nicest mountain
    Are awfully long.

4. LAKES

(For Isaiah Berlin)

A lake allows an average father, walking slowly,
  To circumvent it in an afternoon,
And any healthy mother to halloo the children
  Back to her bedtime from their games across:
(Anything bigger than that, like Michigan or Baikal,
  Though potable, is an 'estranging sea').

Lake-folk require no fiend to keep them on their toes;
  They leave aggression to ill-bred romantics
Who duel with their shadows over blasted heaths:
  A month in a lacustrine atmosphere
Would find the fluvial rivals waltzing not exchanging
  The rhyming insults of their great-great-uncles.

No wonder Christendom did not get really started
  Till, scarred by torture, white from caves and jails,
Her pensive chiefs converged on the Ascanian Lake
  And by that stork-infested shore invented
The life of Godhead, making catholic the figure
  Of three small fishes in a triangle.

Sly Foreign Ministers should always meet beside one,
  For, whether they walk widdershins or deasil,
The path will yoke their shoulders to one liquid centre
  Like two old donkeys pumping as they plod;
Such physical compassion may not guarantee
  A marriage for their armies, but it helps.

Only a very wicked or conceited man,
  About to sink somewhere in mid-Atlantic,
Could think Poseidon's frown was meant for him in person,
  But it is only human to believe
The little lady of the glacier lake has fallen
  In love with the rare bather whom she drowns.

The drinking water of the city where one panics
  At nothing noticing how real one is
May come from reservoirs whose guards are all too conscious
  Of being followed: Webster's cardinal
Saw in a fish-pool something horrid with a hay-rake;
  I know a Sussex hammer-pond like that.

A haunted lake is sick, though; normally, they doctor
  Our tactile fevers with a visual world
Where beaks are dumb like boughs and faces calm like houses;
  The water-scorpion finds it quite unticklish,

261

And, if it shudder slightly when caressed by boats,
  It never asks for water or a loan.

Liking one's Nature, as lake-lovers do, benign
  Goes with a wish for savage dogs and man-traps:
One Fall, one dispossession, is enough, I'm sorry;
  Why should I give Lake Eden to the Nation
Just because every mortal Jack and Jill has been
  The genius of some amniotic mere?

It is unlikely I shall ever keep a swan
  Or build a tower on any small tombolo,
But that's not going to stop me wondering what sort
  Of lake I would decide on if I should.
Moraine, pot, oxbow, glint, sink, crater, piedmont, dimple . . .?
  Just reeling off their names is ever so comfy.

5. ISLANDS

(For Giovanni Maresca)

Old saints on millstones float with cats
  To islands out at sea
Whereon no female pelvis can
  Threaten their agape.

Beyond the long arm of the Law,
  Close to a shipping road,
Pirates in their island lairs
  Observe the pirate code.

Obsession with security
  In Sovereigns prevails;
His Highness and The People both
  Pick islands for their jails.

Once, where detected worldlings now
  Do penitential jobs,
Exterminated species played
  Who had not read their Hobbes.

His continental damage done,
    Laid on an island shelf,
Napoleon has five years more
    To talk about himself.

How fascinating is that class
    Whose only member is Me!
Sappho, Tiberius and I
    Hold forth beside the sea.

What is cosier than the shore
    Of a lake turned inside out?
How do all these other people
    Dare to be about?

In democratic nudity
    Their sexes lie; except
By age or weight you could not tell
    The keeping from the kept.

They go, she goes, thou goest, I go
    To a mainland livelihood:
Farmer and fisherman complain
    The other has it good.

6. PLAINS

(For Wendell Johnson)

I can imagine quite easily ending up
    In a decaying port on a desolate coast,
Cadging drinks from the unwary, a quarrelsome,
    Disreputable old man; I can picture
A second childhood in a valley, scribbling
    Reams of edifying and unreadable verse;
But I cannot see a plain without a shudder;
    'O God, please, please, don't ever make me live there!'

It's horrible to think what peaks come down to,
    That pecking rain and squelching glacier defeat
Tall pomps of stone where goddesses lay sleeping,
    Dreaming of being woken by some chisel's kiss,
That what those blind brutes leave when they are through is
        nothing
    But a mere substance, a clay that meekly takes
The potter's cuff, a gravel that as concrete
    Will unsex any space which it encloses.

And think of growing where all elsewheres are equal!
    So long as there's a hill-ridge somewhere the dreamer
Can place his land of marvels; in poor valleys
    Orphans can head downstream to seek a million:
Here nothing points; to choose between Art and Science
    An embryo genius would have to spin a stick.
What could these farms do if set loose but drift like clouds,
    What goal of unrest is there but the Navy?

Romance? Not in this weather. Ovid's charmer
    Who leads the quadrilles in Arcady, boy-lord
Of hearts who can call their Yes and No their own,
    Would, madcap that he is, soon die of cold or sunstroke:
These lives are in firmer hands; that old grim She
    Who makes the blind dates for the hatless genera
Creates their country matters. (Woe to the child-bed,
    Woe to the strawberries if She's in Her moods!)

And on these attend, greedy as fowl and harsher
    Than any climate, Caesar with all his They.
If a tax-collector disappear in the hills,
    If, now and then, a keeper is shot in the forest,
No thunder follows, but where roads run level,
    How swift to the point of protest strides the Crown.
It hangs, it flogs, it fines, it goes. There is drink.
    There are wives to beat. But Zeus is with the strong,

Born as a rule in some small place (an island,
    Quite often, where a smart lad can spot the bluff

Whence cannon would put the harbour at his mercy),
  Though it is here they chamber with Clio. At this brook
The Christian cross-bow stopped the Heathen scimitar;
  Here is a windmill whence an emperor saw
His right wing crumple; across these cabbage fields
  A pretender's Light Horse made their final charge.

If I were a plainsman I should hate us all,
  From the mechanic rioting for a cheap loaf
To the fastidious palate, hate the painter
  Who steals my wrinkles for his Twelve Apostles,
Hate the priest who cannot even make it shower.
  What could I smile at as I trudged behind my harrow
But bloodshot images of rivers howling,
  Marbles in panic, and Don't-Care made to care?

As it is, though, I know them personally
  Only as a landscape common to two nightmares:
Across them, spotted by spiders from afar,
  I have tried to run, knowing there was no hiding and no help;
On them, in brilliant moonlight, I have lost my way
  And stood without a shadow at the dead centre
Of an abominable desolation,
  Like Tarquin ravished by his post-coital sadness.

Which goes to show I've reason to be frightened
  Not of plains, of course, but of me. I should like
— Who wouldn't? — to shoot beautifully and be obeyed,
  (I should also like to own a cave with two exits);
I wish I weren't so silly. Though I can't pretend
  To think these flats poetic, it's as well at times
To be reminded that nothing is lovely,
  Not even in poetry, which is not the case.

7. STREAMS

(For Elizabeth Drew)

Dear water, clear water, playful in all your streams,
as you dash or loiter through life who does not love
    to sit beside you, to hear you and see you,
  pure being, perfect in music and movement?

Air is boastful at times, earth slovenly, fire rude,
but you in your bearing are always immaculate,
    the most well-spoken of all the older
  servants in the household of Mrs. Nature.

Nobody suspects you of mocking him, for you still
use the same vocables you were using the day
    before that unexpected row which
  downed every hod on half-finished Babel,

and still talk to yourself: nowhere are you disliked;
arching your torso, you dive from a basalt sill,
    canter across white chalk, slog forward
  through red marls, the aboriginal pilgrim,

at home in all sections, but for whom we should be
idolaters of a single rock, kept apart
    by our landscapes, excluding as alien
  the tales and diets of all other strata.

How could we love the absent one if you did not keep
coming from a distance, or quite directly assist,
    as when past Iseult's tower you floated
  the willow pash-notes of wanted Tristram?

And *Homo Ludens*, surely, is your child, who make
fun of our feuds by opposing identical banks,
    transferring the loam from Huppim
  to Muppim and back each time you crankle.

Growth cannot add to your song: as unchristened brooks
already you whisper to ants what, as Brahma's son,
    descending his titanic staircase
  into Assam, to Himalayan bears you thunder.

And not even man can spoil you: his company
coarsens roses and dogs but, should he herd you through a sluice
    to toil at a turbine, or keep you
  leaping in gardens for his amusement,

innocent still is your outcry, water, and there
even, to his soiled heart raging at what it is,
    tells of a sort of world, quite other,
  altogether different from this one

with its envies and passports, a polis like that
to which, in the name of scholars everywhere,
    Gaston Paris pledged his allegiance
  as Bismarck's siege-guns came within earshot.

Lately, in that dale of all Yorkshire's the loveliest,
where, off its fell-side helter-skelter, Kisdon Beck
    jumps into Swale with a boyish shouting,
  sprawled out on grass, I dozed for a second,

and found myself following a croquet tournament
in a calm enclosure, with thrushes popular:
    of all the players in that cool valley
  the best with the mallet was my darling.

While, on the wolds that begirdled it, wild old men
hunted with spades and hammers, monomaniac each,
    for a megalith or a fossil,
  and bird-watchers crept through mossy beech-woods.

Suddenly, over the lawn we started to run
for, lo, through the trees, in a cream and golden coach
    drawn by two baby locomotives,
  the god of mortal doting approached us,

flanked by his bodyguard, those hairy armigers in green
who laugh at thunderstorms and weep at a blue sky:
    He thanked us for our cheers of homage,
    and promised X and Y a passion undying.

With a wave of his torch he commanded a dance;
so round in a ring we flew, my dear on my right,
    when I awoke. But fortunate seemed that
    day because of my dream and enlightened,

and dearer, water, than ever your voice, as if
glad — though goodness knows why — to run with the human
      race,
    wishing, I thought, the least of men their
    figures of splendour, their holy places.

Shorts

IN MEMORIAM L K-A. 1950–1952

At peace under this mandarin, sleep, Lucina,
Blue-eyed Queen of white cats: for you the Ischian wave shall
    weep
When we who now miss you are American dust, and steep
Epomeo in peace and war augustly a grave-watch keep.

*   *   *

EPITAPH FOR THE UNKNOWN SOLDIER

    To save your world, you asked this man to die:
    Would this man, could he see you now, ask why?

*   *   *

O where would those choleric boys,
Our political orators be,
Were one to deprive them of all
Their igneous figures of speech,
If, instead of stamping out flames
Or consuming stubble with fire,
They could only shut out a draught
Or let in a little fresh air?

* * *

Behold the manly mesomorph
Showing his bulging biceps off,
Whom social workers love to touch,
Though the loveliest girls do not care for him much.

Pretty to watch with bat or ball,
An Achilles, too, in a bar-room brawl,
But in the ditch of hopeless odds,
The hour of desertion by brass and gods,

Not a hero. It is the pink-and-white,
Fastidious, almost girlish, in the night
When the proud-arsed broad-shouldered break and run,
Who covers their retreat, dies at his gun.

* * *

Give me a doctor, partridge-plump,
Short in the leg and broad in the rump,
An endomorph with gentle hands,
Who'll never make absurd demands
That I abandon all my vices,
Nor pull a long face in a crisis,
But with a twinkle in his eye
Will tell me that I have to die.

* * *

Fair is Middle-Earth nor changes, though to Age,
Raging at his uncomeliness,
Her wine turn sour, her bread tasteless.

* * *

A Young Person came out of the mists,
Who had the most beautiful wrists:
    A scandal occurred
    Which has long been interred,
But the legend about them persists.

* * *

As the poets have mournfully sung,
Death takes the innocent young,
    The rolling in money,
    The screamingly funny,
And those who are very well hung.

* * *

Guard, Civility, with guns
Your modes and your declensions:
Any lout can spear with ease
Singular Archimedes.

* * *

Bull-roarers cannot keep up the annual rain,
The water-table of a once green champaign
Sinks, will keep on sinking: but why complain? Against odds,
Methods of dry-farming shall still produce grain.

* * *

From bad lands where eggs are small and dear,
Climbing to worse by a stonier
Track, when all are spent we hear it: — the right song
For the wrong time of year.

Five Songs

I

Deftly, admiral, cast your fly
   Into the slow deep hover,
Till the wise old trout mistake and die;
   Salt are the deeps that cover
    The glittering fleets you led,
     White is your head.

Read on, ambassador, engrossed
   In your favourite Stendhal;
The Outer Provinces are lost,
   Unshaven horsemen swill
    The great wines of the Chateaux
     Where you danced long ago.

Do not turn, do not lift your eyes
   Toward the still pair standing
On the bridge between your properties,
   Indifferent to your minding:
    In its glory, in its power,
     This is their hour.

Nothing your strength, your skill, could do
   Can alter their embrace
Or dispersuade the Furies who
   At the appointed place
    With claw and dreadful brow
     Wait for them now.

II

The Emperor's favourite concubine
   Was in the Eunuch's pay,
The Wardens of the Marches turned
   Their spears the other way;

The vases crack, the ladies die,
    The Oracles are wrong:
We suck our thumbs or sleep; the show
    Is gamey and too long.

But — Music Ho! — at last it comes,
    The Transformation Scene:
A rather scruffy-looking god
    Descends in a machine
And, gabbling off his rustic rhymes,
    Misplacing one or two,
Commands the prisoners to walk,
    The enemies to screw.

III

A starling and a willow-wren
    On a may-tree by a weir
Saw them meet and heard him say;
    'Dearest of my dear,
More lively than these waters chortling
    As they leap the dam,
My sweetest duck, my precious goose,
    My white lascivious lamb.'
With a smile she listened to him,
    Talking to her there:
What does he want? said the willow-wren;
    Much too much, said the stare.

'Forgive these loves who dwell in me,
    These brats of greed and fear,
The honking bottom-pinching clown,
    The snivelling sonneteer,
That so, between us, even these,
    Who till the grave are mine,
For all they fall so short of may,
    Dear heart, be still a sign.'
With a smile she closed her eyes,
    Silent she lay there:

Does he mean what he says? said the willow-wren;
    Some of it, said the stare.

'Hark! Wild Robin winds his horn
    And, as his notes require,
Now our laughter-loving spirits
    Must in awe retire
And let their kinder partners,
    Speechless with desire,
Go in their holy selfishness,
    Unfunny to the fire.'
Smiling, silently she threw
    Her arms about him there:
Is it only that? said the willow-wren;
    It's that as well, said the stare.

Waking in her arms he cried,
    Utterly content;
'I have heard the high good noises,
    Promoted for an instant,
Stood upon the shining outskirts
    Of that Joy I thank
For you, my dog and every goody.'
    There on the grass bank
She laughed, he laughed, they laughed together,
    Then they ate and drank:
Did he know what he meant? said the willow-wren—
    God only knows, said the stare.

IV

'When rites and melodies begin
    To alter modes and times,
And timid bar-flies boast aloud
    Of uncommitted crimes,
And leading families are proud
    To dine with their black sheep,
What promises, what discipline,
    If any, will Love keep?'

So roared Fire on their right:
　　But Tamino and Pamina
　　Walked past its rage,
　Sighing O, sighing O,
In timeless fermatas of awe and delight
　　(Innocent? Yes. Ignorant? No.)
　　Down the grim passage.

'When stinking Chaos lifts the latch,
　And Grotte backward spins,
And Helen's nose becomes a beak,
　And cats and dogs grow chins,
And daisies claw and pebbles shriek,
　And Form and Colour part,
What swarming hatreds then will hatch
　Out of Love's riven heart?'
　　So hissed Water on their left:
　　But Pamina and Tamino
　　Opposed its spite,
　With his worship, with her sweetness —
O look now! See how they emerge from the cleft
　　(Frightened? No. Happy? Yes.)
　　Out into sunlight.

V

Make this night loveable,
Moon, and with eye single
Looking down from up there
Bless me, One especial,
And friends everywhere.

With a cloudless brightness
Surround our absences;
Innocent be our sleeps,
Watched by great still spaces,
White hills, glittering deeps.

Parted by circumstance,
Grant each your indulgence
That we may meet in dreams
For talk, for dalliance,
By warm hearths, by cool streams.

Shine lest tonight any,
In the dark suddenly,
Wake alone in a bed
To hear his own fury
Wishing his love were dead.

Three Occasional Poems

I. TO T. S. ELIOT
ON HIS SIXTIETH BIRTHDAY. (1948)

When things began to happen to our favourite spot,
a key missing, a library bust defaced,
    then on the tennis-court one morning,
   outrageous, the bloody corpse, and always,

blank day after day, the unheard-of drought, it was you
who, not speechless from shock but finding the right
    language for thirst and fear, did much to
   prevent a panic. It is the crime that

counts, you will say. We know, but would gratefully add,
to-day as we wait for the Law to take its course
    (and which of us shall escape whipping?),
   that your sixty years have not been wasted.

II. METALOGUE TO THE MAGIC FLUTE

Relax, Maestro, put your baton down:
Only the fogiest of the old will frown
If you the trials of the *Prince* prorogue
To let *Sarastro* speak this Metalogue,
A form acceptable to us, although
Unclassed by *Aristotle* or *Boileau*.
No modern audience finds it incorrect,
For interruption is what we expect
Since that new god, the Paid Announcer, rose,
Who with his quasi-Ossianic prose
Cuts in upon the lovers, halts the band,
To name a sponsor or to praise a brand.
Not that I have a product to describe
That you could wear or cook with or imbibe;
You cannot hoard or waste a work of art:
I come to praise but not to sell *Mozart*,
Who came into this world of war and woe
At Salzburg just two centuries ago,
When kings were many and machines were few
And open Atheism something new.
(It makes a servantless New Yorker sore
To think sheer Genius had to stand before
A mere Archbishop with uncovered head:
But *Mozart* never had to make his bed.)

The history of Music as of Man
Will not go cancrizans, and no ear can
Recall what, when the Archduke *Francis* reigned,
Was heard by ears whose treasure-hoard contained
A *Flute* already but as yet no *Ring*;
Each age has its own mode of listening.
We know the *Mozart* of our fathers' time
Was gay, rococo, sweet, but not sublime,
A Viennese Italian; that is changed
Since music critics learned to feel 'estranged';

Now it's the Germans he is classed amongst,
A *Geist* whose music was composed from *Angst*,
At International Festivals enjoys
An equal status with the Twelve-Tone Boys;
He awes the lovely and the very rich,
And even those *Divertimenti* which
He wrote to play while bottles were uncorked,
Milord chewed noisily, Milady talked,
Are heard in solemn silence, score on knees,
Like quartets by the deafest of the *B's*.
What next? One can no more imagine how,
In concert halls two hundred years from now,
When the mozartian sound-waves move the air,
The cognoscenti will be moved, than dare
Predict how high orchestral pitch will go,
How many tones will constitute a row,
The tempo at which regimented feet
Will march about the Moon, the form of Suite
For Piano in a Post-Atomic Age,
Prepared by some contemporary *Cage*.

An opera composer may be vexed
By later umbrage taken at his text:
Even *Macaulay's* schoolboy knows to-day
What *Robert Graves* or *Margaret Mead* would say
About the status of the sexes in this play,
Writ in that era of barbaric dark
'Twixt Modern Mom and Bronze-Age Matriarch.
Where now the Roman Fathers and their creed?
'Ah, where,' sighs *Mr. Mitty*, 'where indeed?',
And glances sideways at his vital spouse
Whose rigid jaw-line and contracted brows
Express her scorn and utter detestation
For Roman views of Female Education.

In Nineteen-Fifty-Six we find the *Queen*
A highly-paid and most efficient Dean
(Who, as we all know, really runs the College),
Sarastro, tolerated for his knowledge,

Teaching the History of Ancient Myth
At *Bryn Mawr, Vassar, Bennington* or *Smith*;
Pamina may a *Time* researcher be
To let *Tamino* take his Ph.D.,
Acquiring manly wisdom as he wishes
While changing diapers and doing dishes;
Sweet *Papagena*, when she's time to spare,
Listens to *Mozart* operas on the air,
Though *Papageno*, we are sad to feel,
Prefers the juke-box to the glockenspiel,
And how is — what was easy in the past —
A democratic villain to be cast?
Monostatos must make his bad impression
Without a race, religion or profession.

A work that lasts two hundred years is tough,
And operas, God knows, must stand enough:
What greatness made, small vanities abuse.
What must they not endure? The Diva whose
Fioriture and climactic note
The silly old composer never wrote,
Conductor *X*, that over-rated bore
Who alters tempi and who cuts the score,
Director *Y* who with ingenious wit
Places his wretched singers in the pit
While dancers mime their roles, *Z* the Designer
Who sets the whole thing on an ocean liner,
The girls in shorts, the men in yachting caps;
Yet Genius triumphs over all mishaps,
Survives a greater obstacle than these,
Translation into foreign Operese
(English sopranos are condemned to *languish*
Because our tenors have to hide their *anguish*);
It soothes the *Frank*, it stimulates the *Greek*:
Genius surpasses all things, even Chic.
We who know nothing — which is just as well —
About the future, can, at least, foretell,
Whether they live in air-borne nylon cubes,
Practise group-marriage or are fed through tubes,

278

That crowds two centuries from now will press
(Absurd their hair, ridiculous their dress)
And pay in currencies, however weird,
To hear *Sarastro* booming through his beard,
Sharp connoisseurs approve if it is clean
The F in alt of the *Nocturnal Queen*,
Some uncouth creature from the *Bronx* amaze
Park Avenue by knowing all the *K*'s.

How seemly, then, to celebrate the birth
Of one who did no harm to our poor earth,
Created masterpieces by the dozen,
Indulged in toilet humour with his cousin,
And had a pauper's funeral in the rain,
The like of whom we shall not see again:
How comely, also, to forgive; we should,
As *Mozart*, were he living, surely would,
Remember kindly *Salieri's* shade,
Accused of murder and his works unplayed,
Nor, while we praise the dead, should we forget
We have *Stravinsky* — bless him! — with us yet.
⎧*Basta*! Maestro, make your minions play!
⎨In all hearts, as in our finale, may
⎩Reason & Love be crowned, assume their rightful sway.

III

*Lines addressed to Dr. Claude Jenkins, Canon of Christ Church,
Oxford, on the occasion of his Eightieth Birthday. (May 26th, 1957)*

Let both our Common Rooms combine to cheer
This day when you complete your eightieth year,
The tribes who study and the sporting clan
Applaud the scholar and approve the man,
While, in cold *Mercury*, complacent fish
From well-fed tummies belch a birthday wish.
Long may you see a congregation sit
Enraptured by your piety and wit,

{ At many a luncheon feed us from your store
{ Of curious fact and anecdotal lore
{ (Why! even *Little* knows but little more):
And when at last your eager soul shall fly
(As do all Canons of the *House*) on high,
May you find all things to your liking there,
A warmer Canonry await you where
Nor dry-rot shall corrupt, nor moisture rust,
Nor froward *Censor* dare break in to dust,
Celestial rooms where you may talk with men
Like *St. Augustine*, *Duchesne*, *Origen*,
While Seraphim purvey immortal snuff,
More pungent than our mere sub-lunar stuff,
Baroquish Cherubim cry: — 'Glory, Laud,
Eternal Honour to our *Dr. Claude*!'

Their Lonely Betters

As I listened from a beach-chair in the shade
To all the noises that my garden made,
It seemed to me only proper that words
Should be withheld from vegetables and birds.

A robin with no Christian name ran through
The Robin-Anthem which was all it knew,
And rustling flowers for some third party waited
To say which pairs, if any, should get mated.

No one of them was capable of lying,
There was not one which knew that it was dying
Or could have with a rhythm or a rhyme
Assumed responsibility for time.

Let them leave language to their lonely betters
Who count some days and long for certain letters;
We, too, make noises when we laugh or weep:
Words are for those with promises to keep.

First Things First

Woken, I lay in the arms of my own warmth and listened
To a storm enjoying its storminess in the winter dark
Till my ear, as it can when half-asleep or half-sober,
Set to work to unscramble that interjectory uproar,
Construing its airy vowels and watery consonants
Into a love-speech indicative of a Proper Name.

Scarcely the tongue I should have chosen, yet, as well
As harshness and clumsiness would allow, it spoke in your praise,
Kenning you a god-child of the Moon and the West Wind
With power to tame both real and imaginary monsters,
Likening your poise of being to an upland county,
Here green on purpose, there pure blue for luck.

Loud though it was, alone as it certainly found me,
It reconstructed a day of peculiar silence
When a sneeze could be heard a mile off, and had me walking
On a headland of lava beside you, the occasion as ageless
As the stare of any rose, your presence exactly
So once, so valuable, so very now.

This, moreover, at an hour when only too often
A smirking devil annoys me in beautiful English,
Predicting a world where every sacred location
Is a sand-buried site all cultured Texans do,
Misinformed and thoroughly fleeced by their guides,
And gentle hearts are extinct like Hegelian Bishops.

Grateful, I slept till a morning that would not say
How much it believed of what I said the storm had said
But quietly drew my attention to what had been done
— So many cubic metres the more in my cistern
Against a leonine summer —, putting first things first:
Thousands have lived without love, not one without water.

The More Loving One

Looking up at the stars, I know quite well
That, for all they care, I can go to hell,
But on earth indifference is the least
We have to dread from man or beast.

How should we like it were stars to burn
With a passion for us we could not return?
If equal affection cannot be,
Let the more loving one be me.

Admirer as I think I am
Of stars that do not give a damn,
I cannot, now I see them, say
I missed one terribly all day.

Were all stars to disappear or die,
I should learn to look at an empty sky
And feel its total dark sublime,
Though this might take me a little time.

A Permanent Way

Self-drivers may curse their luck,
Stuck on new-fangled trails,
But the good old train will jog
To the dogma of its rails,

And steam so straight ahead
That I cannot be led astray
By tempting scenes which occur
Along any permanent way.

Intriguing dales escape
Into hills of the shape I like,
Though, were I actually put
Where a foot-path leaves the pike

For some steep romantic spot,
I should ask what chance there is
Of at least a ten-dollar cheque
Or a family peck of a kiss:

But, forcibly held to my tracks,
I can safely relax and dream
Of a love and a livelihood
To fit that wood or stream;

And what could be greater fun,
Once one has chosen and paid,
Than the inexpensive delight
Of a choice one might have made?

Nocturne

Appearing unannounced, the moon
Avoids a mountain's jagged prongs
And sweeps into the open sky
Like one who knows where she belongs.

To me, immediately, my heart:
'Adore Her, Mother, Virgin, Muse,
A Face worth watching Who can make
Or break you as Her fancy choose.'

At which the reflex of my mind:
'You will not tell me, I presume,
That bunch of barren craters care
Who sleeps with or who tortures whom.'

Tonight, like umpteen other nights,
The baser frankness wins of course,
My tougher mind which dares admit
That both are worshippers of force.

Granted what both of them believe,
The Goddess, clearly, has to go,
Whose majesty is but the mask
That hides a faceless dynamo;

And neither of my natures can
Complain if I should be reduced
To a small functionary whose dreams
Are vast, unscrupulous, confused.

Supposing, though, my face is real
And not a myth or a machine,
The moon should look like x and wear
Features I've actually seen,

My neighbour's face, a face as such,
Neither a status nor a sex,
Constant for me no matter what
The value I assign to x;

That gushing lady, possibly,
Who brought some verses of her own,
That hang-dog who keeps coming back
For just a temporary loan;

A counter-image, anyway,
To balance with its lack of weight
My world, the private motor-car
And all the engines of the State.

Precious Five

Be patient, solemn nose,
Serve in a world of prose
The present moment well,
Nor surlily contrast
Its brash ill-mannered smell
With grand scents of the past.
That calm enchanted wood,
That grave world where you stood
So gravely at its middle,
Its oracle and riddle,
Has all been altered; now
In anxious times you serve
As bridge from mouth to brow,
An asymmetric curve
Thrust outward from a face
Time-conscious into space,
Whose oddness may provoke
To a mind-saving joke
A mind that would it were
An apathetic sphere:
Point, then, for honour's sake
Up the storm-beaten slope
From memory to hope
The way you cannot take.

Be modest, lively ears,
Spoiled darlings of a stage
Where any caper cheers
The paranoiac mind
Of this undisciplined
And concert-going age,
So lacking in conviction
It cannot take pure fiction,
And what it wants from you
Are rumours partly true;
Before you catch its sickness
Submit your lucky quickness

And levity to rule,
Go back again to school,
Drudge patiently until
No whisper is too much
And your precision such
At any sound that all
Seem natural, not one
Fantastic or banal,
And then do what you will:
Dance with angelic grace,
In ecstasy and fun,
The luck you cannot place.

Be civil, hands; on you
Although you cannot read
Is written what you do
And blows you struck so blindly
In temper or in greed,
Your tricks of long ago,
Eyes, kindly or unkindly,
Unknown to you will know.
Revere those hairy wrists
And leg-of-mutton fists
Which pulverised the trolls
And carved deep Donts in stone,
Great hands which under knolls
Are now disjointed bone,
But what has been has been;
A tight arthritic claw
Or aldermanic paw
Waving about in praise
Of those homeric days
Is impious and obscene:
Grow, hands, into those living
Hands which true hands should be
By making and by giving
To hands you cannot see.

Look, naked eyes, look straight
At all eyes but your own
Lest in a tête-à-tête
Of glances double-crossed,
Both knowing and both known,
Your nakedness be lost;
Rove curiously about
But look from inside out,
Compare two eyes you meet
By dozens on the street,
One shameless, one ashamed,
Too lifeless to be blamed,
With eyes met now and then
Looking from living men,
Which in petrarchan fashion
Play opposite the heart,
Their humour to her passion,
Her nature to their art,
For mutual undeceiving;
True seeing is believing
(What sight can never prove)
There is a world to see:
Look outward, eyes, and love
Those eyes you cannot be.

Praise, tongue, the Earthly Muse
By number and by name
In any style you choose,
For nimble tongues and lame
Have both found favour; praise
Her port and sudden ways,
Now fish-wife and now queen,
Her reason and unreason:
Though freed from that machine,
Praise Her revolving wheel
Of appetite and season
In honour of Another,
The old self you become
At any drink or meal,

That animal of taste,
And of his twin, your brother,
Unlettered, savage, dumb,
Down there below the waist:
Although your style be fumbling,
Half stutter and half song,
Give thanks however bumbling,
Telling for Her dear sake
To whom all styles belong
The truth She cannot make.

Be happy, precious five,
So long as I'm alive
Nor try to ask me what
You should be happy for;
Think, if it helps, of love
Or alcohol or gold,
But do as you are told.
I could (which you cannot)
Find reasons fast enough
To face the sky and roar
In anger and despair
At what is going on,
Demanding that it name
Whoever is to blame:
The sky would only wait
Till all my breath was gone
And then reiterate
As if I wasn't there
That singular command
I do not understand,
Bless what there is for being,
Which has to be obeyed, for
What else am I made for,
Agreeing or disagreeing?

Memorial for the City

(*In memoriam Charles Williams, d. April* 1945)

In the self-same point that our soul is made sensual, in the self-same point is the City of God ordained to him from without beginning.

JULIANA OF NORWICH

I

The eyes of the crow and the eye of the camera open
Onto Homer's world, not ours. First and last
They magnify earth, the abiding
Mother of gods and men; if they notice either
It is only in passing: gods behave, men die,
Both feel in their own small way, but She
Does nothing and does not care.
She alone is seriously there.

The crow on the crematorium chimney
And the camera roving the battle
Record a space where time has no place.
On the right a village is burning, in a market-town to the left
The soldiers fire, the mayor bursts into tears,
The captives are led away, while far in the distance
A tanker sinks into a dedolant sea.
That is the way things happen; for ever and ever
Plum-blossom falls on the dead, the roar of the waterfall covers
The cries of the whipped and the sighs of the lovers
And the hard bright light composes
A meaningless moment into an eternal fact
Which a whistling messenger disappears with into a defile:
One enjoys glory, one endures shame;
He may, she must. There is no one to blame.

The steady eyes of the crow and the camera's candid eye
See as honestly as they know how, but they lie.
The crime of life is not time. Even now, in this night
Among the ruins of the Post-Vergilian City
Where our past is a chaos of graves and the barbed-wire stretches
  ahead

Into our future till it is lost to sight,
Our grief is not Greek: As we bury our dead
We know without knowing there is reason for what we bear,
That our hurt is not a desertion, that we are to pity
Neither ourselves nor our city;
Whoever the searchlights catch, whatever the loudspeakers blare,
We are not to despair.

II

Alone in a room Pope Gregory whispered his name
    While the Emperor shone on a centreless world
From wherever he happened to be; the New City rose
    Upon their opposition, the yes and no
Of a rival allegiance; the sword, the local lord
    Were not all; there was home and Rome;
Fear of the stranger was lost on the way to the shrine.

The facts, the acts of the City bore a double meaning:
    Limbs became hymns; embraces expressed in jest
A more permanent tie; infidel faces replaced
    The family foe in the choleric's nightmare;
The children of water parodied in their postures
    The infinite patience of heaven;
Those born under Saturn felt the gloom of the day of doom.

Scribes and innkeepers prospered; suspicious tribes combined
    To rescue Jerusalem from a dull god,
And disciplined logicians fought to recover thought
    From the eccentricities of the private brain
For the Sane City; framed in her windows, orchards, ports,
    Wild beasts, deep rivers and dry rocks
Lay nursed on the smile of a merciful Madonna.

In a sandy province Luther denounced as obscene
    The machine that so smoothly forgave and saved
If paid; he announced to the Sinful City a grinning gap
    No rite could cross; he abased her before the Grace:

Henceforth division was also to be her condition;
   Her conclusions were to include doubt,
Her loves were to bear with her fear; insecure, she endured.

Saints tamed, poets acclaimed the raging herod of the will;
   The groundlings wept as on a secular stage
The grand and the bad went to ruin in thundering verse;
   Sundered by reason and treason the City
Found invisible ground for concord in measured sound,
   While wood and stone learned the shameless
Games of man, to flatter, to show off, be pompous, to romp.

Nature was put to the Question in the Prince's name;
   She confessed, what he wished to hear, that she had no soul;
Between his scaffold and her coldness the restrained style,
   The ironic smile became the worldly and devout,
Civility a city grown rich: in his own snob way
   The unarmed gentleman did his job
As a judge to her children, as a father to her forests.

In a national capital Mirabeau and his set
   Attacked mystery; the packed galleries roared
And history marched to the drums of a clear idea,
   The aim of the Rational City, quick to admire,
Quick to tire: she used up Napoleon and threw him away;
   Her pallid affected heroes
Began their hectic quest for the prelapsarian man.

The deserts were dangerous, the waters rough, their clothes
   Absurd but, changing their Beatrices often,
Sleeping little, they pushed on, raised the flag of the Word
   Upon lawless spots denied or forgotten
By the fear or the pride of the Glittering City;
   Guided by hated parental shades,
They invaded and harrowed the hell of her natural self.

Chimeras mauled them, they wasted away with the spleen,
   Suicide picked them off; sunk off Cape Consumption,
Lost on the Tosspot Seas, wrecked on the Gibbering Isles
   Or trapped in the ice of despair at the Soul's Pole,

They died, unfinished, alone; but now the forbidden,
  The hidden, the wild outside were known:
Faithful without faith, they died for the Conscious City.

III

    Across the square,
Between the burnt-out Law Courts and Police Headquarters,
Past the Cathedral far too damaged to repair,
Around the Grand Hotel patched up to hold reporters,
    Near huts of some Emergency Committee,
    The barbed wire runs through the abolished City.

    Across the plains,
Between two hills, two villages, two trees, two friends,
The barbed wire runs which neither argues nor explains
But, where it likes, a place, a path, a railroad ends,
    The humour, the cuisine, the rites, the taste,
    The pattern of the City, are erased.

    Across our sleep
The barbed wire also runs: It trips us so we fall
And white ships sail without us though the others weep,
It makes our sorry fig-leaf at the Sneerers' Ball,
    It ties the smiler to the double bed,
    It keeps on growing from the witch's head.

    Behind the wire
Which is behind the mirror, our Image is the same
Awake or dreaming: It has no image to admire,
No age, no sex, no memory, no creed, no name,
    It can be counted, multiplied, employed
    In any place, at any time destroyed.

    Is it our friend?
No; that is our hope; that we weep and It does not grieve,
That for It the wire and the ruins are not the end:
This is the flesh we are but never would believe,
    The flesh we die but it is death to pity;
    This is Adam waiting for His City.

Let Our Weakness speak

IV

Without me Adam would have fallen irrevocably with Lucifer;
    he would never have been able to cry *O felix culpa*.
It was I who suggested his theft to Prometheus; my frailty cost
    Adonis his life.
I heard Orpheus sing; I was not quite as moved as they say.
I was not taken in by the sheep's-eyes of Narcissus; I was angry
    with Psyche when she struck a light.
I was in Hector's confidence; so far as it went.
Had he listened to me Oedipus would never have left Corinth; I
    cast no vote at the trial of Orestes.
I fell asleep when Diotima spoke of love; I was not responsible for
    the monsters which tempted St. Anthony.
To me the Saviour permitted His Fifth Word from the cross; to be
    a stumbling-block to the stoics.
I was the unwelcome third at the meetings of Tristan with Isolda;
    they tried to poison me.
I rode with Galahad on his Quest for the San Graal; without
    understanding I kept his vow.
I was the just impediment to the marriage of Faustus with Helen;
    I know a ghost when I see one.
With Hamlet I had no patience; but I forgave Don Quixote all for
    his admission in the cart.
I was the missing entry in Don Giovanni's list; for which he could
    never account.
I assisted Figaro the Barber in all his intrigues; when Prince
    Tamino arrived at wisdom I too obtained my reward.
I was innocent of the sin of the Ancient Mariner; time after time I
    warned Captain Ahab to accept happiness.
As for Metropolis, that too-great city; her delusions are not mine.
Her speeches impress me little, her statistics less; to all who dwell
    on the public side of her mirrors, resentments and no peace.
At the place of my passion her photographers are gathered
    together; but I shall rise again to hear her judged.

The Shield of Achilles

> She looked over his shoulder
>   For vines and olive trees,
> Marble well-governed cities
>   And ships upon untamed seas,
> But there on the shining metal
>   His hands had put instead
> An artificial wilderness
>   And a sky like lead.

A plain without a feature, bare and brown,
    No blade of grass, no sign of neighbourhood,
Nothing to eat and nowhere to sit down,
    Yet, congregated on its blankness, stood
    An unintelligible multitude,
A million eyes, a million boots in line,
Without expression, waiting for a sign.

Out of the air a voice without a face
    Proved by statistics that some cause was just
In tones as dry and level as the place:
    No one was cheered and nothing was discussed;
    Column by column in a cloud of dust
They marched away enduring a belief
Whose logic brought them, somewhere else, to grief.

> She looked over his shoulder
>   For ritual pieties,
> White flower-garlanded heifers,
>   Libation and sacrifice,
> But there on the shining metal
>   Where the altar should have been,
> She saw by his flickering forge-light
>   Quite another scene.

Barbed wire enclosed an arbitrary spot
    Where bored officials lounged (one cracked a joke)

And sentries sweated for the day was hot:
  A crowd of ordinary decent folk
  Watched from without and neither moved nor spoke
As three pale figures were led forth and bound
To three posts driven upright in the ground.

The mass and majesty of this world, all
  That carries weight and always weighs the same
Lay in the hands of others; they were small
  And could not hope for help and no help came:
  What their foes liked to do was done, their shame
Was all the worst could wish; they lost their pride
And died as men before their bodies died.

    She looked over his shoulder
      For athletes at their games,
    Men and women in a dance
      Moving their sweet limbs
    Quick, quick, to music,
      But there on the shining shield
    His hands had set no dancing-floor
      But a weed-choked field.

A ragged urchin, aimless and alone,
  Loitered about that vacancy, a bird
Flew up to safety from his well-aimed stone:
  That girls are raped, that two boys knife a third,
  Were axioms to him, who'd never heard
Of any world where promises were kept,
Or one could weep because another wept.

    The thin-lipped armourer,
      Hephaestos hobbled away,
    Thetis of the shining breasts
      Cried out in dismay
    At what the god had wrought
      To please her son, the strong
    Iron-hearted man-slaying Achilles
      Who would not live long.

Secondary Epic

No, Virgil, no:
Not even the first of the Romans can learn
His Roman history in the future tense,
Not even to serve your political turn;
Hindsight as foresight makes no sense.

How was your shield-making god to explain
Why his masterpiece, his grand panorama
Of scenes from the coming historical drama
Of an unborn nation, war after war,
All the birthdays needed to pre-ordain
The Octavius the world was waiting for,
Should so abruptly, mysteriously stop,
What cause could he show why he didn't foresee
The future beyond 31 B.C.,
Why a curtain of darkness should finally drop
On Carians, Morini, Gelonians with quivers,
Converging Romeward in abject file,
Euphrates, Araxes and similar rivers
Learning to flow in a latinate style,
And Caesar be left where prophecy ends,
Inspecting troops and gifts for ever?
Wouldn't Aeneas have asked: — 'What next?
After this triumph, what portends?'

As rhetoric your device was too clever:
It lets us imagine a continuation
To your Eighth Book, an interpolation,
Scrawled at the side of a tattered text
In a decadent script, the composition
Of a down-at-heels refugee rhetorician
With an empty belly, seeking employment,
Cooked up in haste for the drunken enjoyment
Of some blond princeling whom loot had inclined
To believe that Providence had assigned
To blonds the task of improving mankind.

... *Now Mainz appears and starry New Year's Eve*
As two-horned Rhine throws off the Latin yoke
To bear the Vandal on his frozen back;
Lo! Danube, now congenial to the Goth,
News not unwelcome to Teutonic shades
And all lamenting beyond Acheron
Demolished Carthage or a plundered Greece:
And now Juturna leaves the river-bed
Of her embittered grievance — loud her song,
Immoderate her joy — for word has come
Of treachery at the Salarian Gate.
Alaric has avenged Turnus. ...

No, Virgil, no:
Behind your verse so masterfully made
We hear the weeping of a Muse betrayed.
Your Anchises isn't convincing at all:
It's asking too much of us to be told
A shade so long-sighted, a father who knows
That Romulus will build a wall,
Augustus found an Age of Gold,
And is trying to teach a dutiful son
The love of what will be in the long run,
Would mention them both but not disclose
(Surely, no prophet could afford to miss,
No man of destiny fail to enjoy
So clear a proof of Providence as this.)
The names predestined for the Catholic boy
Whom Arian Odovacer will depose.

Makers of History

Serious historians care for coins and weapons,
Not those re-iterations of one self-importance
By whom they date them,
Knowing that clerks could soon compose a model
As manly as any of whom schoolmasters tell
Their yawning pupils,

With might-be maps of might-have-been campaigns,
Showing in colour the obediences
Before and after,
Quotes from four-letter pep-talks to the troops
And polysyllabic reasons to a Senate
For breaking treaties.

Simple to add how Greatness, incognito,
Admired plain-spoken comment on itself
By Honest John,
And simpler still the phobia, the perversion,
Such curiosa as tease humanistic
Unpolitical palates.

How justly legend melts them into one
Composite demi-god, prodigious worker,
Deflecting rivers,
Walling in cities with his two bare hands,
The burly slave of ritual and a martyr
To Numerology.

With twelve twin brothers, three wives, seven sons,
Five weeks a year he puts on petticoats,
Stung mortally
During a nine-day tussle with King Scorpion,
Dies in the thirteenth month, becomes immortal
As a constellation.

Clio loves those who bred them better horses,
Found answers to their questions, made their things,
Even those fulsome
Bards they boarded: but these mere commanders,
Like boys in pimple-time, like girls at awkward ages,
What did they do but wish?

T The Great

Begot like other children, he
Was known among his kin as T,

A name, like those we never hear of,
Which nobody yet walked in fear of.

One morning when the West awoke,
The rising sun was veiled in smoke,

And fugitives, their horse-hooves drumming,
Cried: — 'Death is on you! T is coming!'

For a considerable season
The name T was sufficient reason

To raise the question (Who can drop it?):
'If God exists, why can't He stop it?',

A synonym in a whole armful
Of languages for what is harmful.

Those, even, who had borne no loss themselves,
If T was spoken of, would cross themselves,

And after he was dead, his traces
Were visible for years — in faces

That wore expressions of alas on them,
And plains without a blade of grass on them.

(Some regions, travellers avow,
Have not recovered even now.)

As earth was starting to breathe freely,
Out of the North, efficient, steely,

Reminding life that hope is vanity,
Came N to bring her back to sanity,

And T was pushed off to the nursery
Before his hundredth anniversary

To play the bogey-man that comes
To naughty boys who suck their thumbs.

After some military success
N died (to be replaced by S)

And took T's job as Kid Detective,
Leaving him wholly ineffective.

For all the harm, and it was quite a lot, he did,
The public could not care less what he did.

(Some scholar cares, we may presume,
But in a Senior Common Room

It is unpopular to throw about
Matters your colleagues do not know about.)

Though T cannot win Clio's cup again,
From time to time the name crops up again,

E.g., as a crossword anagram:
11 Down — A NUBILE TRAM

The Managers

In the bad old days it was not so bad:
   The top of the ladder
Was an amusing place to sit; success
   Meant quite a lot — leisure
And huge meals, more palaces filled with more
   Objects, books, girls, horses
Than one would ever get round to, and to be
   Carried uphill while seeing
Others walk. To rule was a pleasure when
   One wrote a death-sentence

On the back of the Ace of Spades and played on
    With a new deck. Honours
Are not so physical or jolly now,
    For the species of Powers
We are used to are not like that. Could one of them
    Be said to resemble
The Tragic Hero, the Platonic Saint,
    Or would any painter
Portray one rising triumphant from a lake
    On a dolphin, naked,
Protected by an umbrella of cherubs? Can
    They so much as manage
To behave like genuine Caesars when alone
    Or drinking with cronies,
To let their hair down and be frank about
    The world? It is doubtful.
The last word on how we may live or die
    Rests today with such quiet
Men, working too hard in rooms that are too big,
    Reducing to figures
What is the matter, what is to be done.
    A neat little luncheon
Of sandwiches is brought to each on a tray,
    Nourishment they are able
To take with one hand without looking up
    From papers a couple
Of secretaries are needed to file,
    From problems no smiling
Can dismiss. The typewriters never stop
    But whirr like grasshoppers
In the silent siesta heat as, frivolous
    Across their discussions,
From woods unaltered by our wars and our vows
    There drift the scents of flowers
And the songs of birds who will never vote
    Or bother to notice
Those distinguishing marks a lover sees
    By instinct and policemen
Can be trained to observe. Far into the night

Their windows burn brightly
And, behind their backs bent over some report,
   On every quarter,
For ever like a god or a disease
   There on the earth the reason
In all its aspects why they are tired, the weak,
   The inattentive, seeking
Someone to blame. If, to recuperate
   They go a-playing, their greatness
Encounters the bow of the chef or the glance
   Of the ballet-dancer
Who cannot be ruined by any master's fall.
   To rule must be a calling,
It seems, like surgery or sculpture; the fun
   Neither love nor money
But taking necessary risks, the test
   Of one's skill, the question,
If difficult, their own reward. But then
   Perhaps one should mention
Also what must be a comfort as they guess
   In times like the present
When guesses can prove so fatally wrong,
   The fact of belonging
To the very select indeed, to those
   For whom, just supposing
They do, there will be places on the last
   Plane out of disaster.
No; no one is really sorry for their
   Heavy gait and careworn
Look, nor would they thank you if you said you were.

The Epigoni

No use invoking Apollo in a case like theirs;
The pleasure-loving gods had died in their chairs
And would not get up again, one of them, ever,
Though guttural tribes had crossed the Great River,
Roasting their dead and with no name for the yew;

No good expecting long-legged ancestors to
Return with long swords from pelagic paradises
(They would be left to their own devices,
Supposing they had some); no point pretending
One didn't foresee the probable ending
As dog-food, or landless, submerged, a slave:
Meanwhile, how should a cultured gentleman behave?

It would have been an excusable failing
Had they broken out into womanish wailing
Or, dramatising their doom, held forth
In sonorous clap-trap about death;
To their credit, a reader will only perceive
That the language they loved was coming to grief,
Expiring in preposterous mechanical tricks,
Epanaleptics, rhopalics, anacyclic acrostics:
To their lasting honour, the stuff they wrote
Can safely be spanked in a scholar's foot-note,
Called shallow by a mechanised generation to whom
Haphazard oracular grunts are profound wisdom.

Bathtub Thoughts

(c. 500–c. 1950)

Hail, future friend, whose present I
With gratitude now prophesy,
Kind first to whom it shall occur
My past existence to infer.
Brief salutation best beseems
Two nameless ordinal extremes:
Hail and farewell! Chance only knows
The length of our respective rows,
But our numeric bond is such
As gods nor love nor death can touch.

So thought, I thought, the last Romano-Briton
To take his last hot bath.

303

The Old Man's Road

Across the Great Schism, through our whole landscape,
Ignoring God's Vicar and God's Ape,

Under their noses, unsuspected,
The Old Man's Road runs as it did

When a light subsoil, a simple ore
Were still in vogue: true to His wherefore,

By stiles, gates, hedge-gaps it goes
Over ploughland, woodland, cow meadows,

Past shrines to a cosmological myth
No heretic to-day would be caught dead with,

Near hill-top rings that were so safe then,
Now stormed easily by small children

(Shepherds use bits in the high mountains,
Hamlets take stretches for Lovers' Lanes),

Then through cities threads its odd way,
Now without gutters, a Thieves' Alley,

Now with green lamp-posts and white curb,
The smart Crescent of a high-toned suburb,

Giving wide berth to an old Cathedral,
Running smack through a new Town Hall,

Unlookable for, by logic, by guess:
Yet some strike it, and are struck fearless.

No life can know it, but no life
That sticks to this course can be made captive,

And who wander with it are not stopped at
Borders by guards of some Theocrat,

Crossing the pass so almost where
His searchlight squints but no closer

(And no further where it might by chance):
So in summer sometimes, without hindrance,

Apotropaically scowling, a tinker
Shuffles past, in the waning year

Potters a coleopterist, poking
Through yellow leaves, and a youth in spring

Trots by after a new excitement,
His true self, hot on the scent.

The Old Man leaves his Road to those
Who love it no less since it lost purpose,

Who never ask what History is up to,
So cannot act as if they knew:

Assuming a freedom its Powers deny,
Denying its Powers, they pass freely.

The History of Science

All fables of adventure stress
The need for courtesy and kindness:
Without the Helpers none can win
The flaxen-haired Princess.

They look the ones in need of aid,
Yet, thanks to them, the gentle-hearted
Third Brother beds the woken Queen,
While seniors who made

Cantankerous replies to crones
And dogs who begged to share their rations,
Must expiate their pride as daws
Or wind-swept bachelor stones.

Few of a sequel, though, have heard:
Uneasy pedagogues have censored
All written reference to a brother
Younger than the Third.

Soft-spoken as New Moon this Fourth,
A Sun of gifts to all he met with,
But when advised 'Go South a while!',
Smiled 'Thank You!' and turned North,

Trusting some map in his own head,
So never reached the goal intended
(His map, of course, was out) but blundered
On a wonderful instead,

A tower not circular but square,
A treasure not of gold but silver:
He kissed a shorter Sleeper's hand
And stroked her raven hair.

Dare sound Authority confess
That one can err his way to riches,
Win glory by mistake, his dear
Through sheer wrong-headedness?

The History of Truth

In that ago when being was believing,
Truth was the most of many credibles,
More first, more always, than a bat-winged lion,
A fish-tailed dog or eagle-headed fish,
The least like mortals, doubted by their deaths.

Truth was their model as they strove to build
A world of lasting objects to believe in,
Without believing earthernware and legend,
Archway and song, were truthful or untruthful:
The Truth was there already to be true.

This while when, practical like paper-dishes,
Truth is convertible to kilowatts,
Our last to do by is an anti-model,
Some untruth anyone can give the lie to,
A nothing no one need believe is there.

Homage to Clio

Our hill has made its submission and the green
    Swept on into the north: around me,
From morning to night, flowers duel incessantly,
    Colour against colour, in combats

Which they all win, and at any hour from some point else
    May come another tribal outcry
Of a new generation of birds who chirp,
    Not for effect but because chirping

Is the thing to do. More lives than I perceive
    Are aware of mine this May morning
As I sit reading a book, sharper senses
    Keep watch on an inedible patch

Of unsatisfactory smell, unsafe as
    So many areas are: to observation
My book is dead, and by observations they live
    In space, as unaware of silence

As Provocative Aphrodite or her twin,
    Virago Artemis, the Tall Sisters
Whose subjects they are. That is why, in their Dual Realm,
    Banalities can be beautiful,

Why nothing is too big or too small or the wrong
    Colour, and the roar of an earthquake
Rearranging the whispers of streams a loud sound
    Not a din: but we, at haphazard

And unseasonably, are brought face to face
   By ones, Clio, with your silence. After that
Nothing is easy. We may dream as we wish
   Of phallic pillar or navel-stone

With twelve nymphs twirling about it, but pictures
   Are no help: your silence already is there
Between us and any magical centre
   Where things are taken in hand. Besides,

Are we so sorry? Woken at sun-up to hear
   A cock pronouncing himself himself
Though all his sons had been castrated and eaten,
   I was glad I could be unhappy: if

I don't know how I shall manage, at least I know
   The beast-with-two-backs may be a species
Evenly distributed but Mum and Dad
   Were not two other people. To visit

The grave of a friend, to make an ugly scene,
   To count the loves one has grown out of,
Is not nice, but to chirp like a tearless bird,
   As though no one dies in particular

And gossip were never true, unthinkable:
   If it were, forgiveness would be no use,
One-eye-for-one would be just and the innocent
   Would not have to suffer. Artemis,

Aphrodite, are Major Powers and all wise
   Castellans will mind their p's and q's,
But it is you, who never have spoken up,
   Madonna of silences, to whom we turn

When we have lost control, your eyes, Clio, into which
   We look for recognition after
We have been found out. How shall I describe you? They
   Can be represented in granite

(One guesses at once from the perfect buttocks,
    The flawless mouth too grand to have corners,
Whom the colossus must be), but what icon
    Have the arts for you, who look like any

Girl one has not noticed and show no special
    Affinity with a beast? I have seen
Your photo, I think, in the papers, nursing
    A baby or mourning a corpse: each time

You had nothing to say and did not, one could see,
    Observe where you were, Muse of the unique
Historical fact, defending with silence
    Some world of your beholding, a silence

No explosion can conquer but a lover's Yes
    Has been known to fill. So few of the Big
Ever listen: that is why you have a great host
    Of superfluous screams to care for and

Why, up and down like the Duke of Cumberland,
    Or round and round like the Laxey Wheel,
The Short, The Bald, The Pious, The Stammerer went,
    As the children of Artemis go,

Not yours. Lives that obey you move like music,
    Becoming now what they only can be once,
Making of silence decisive sound: it sounds
    Easy, but one must find the time. Clio,

Muse of Time, but for whose merciful silence
    Only the first step would count and that
Would always be murder, whose kindness never
    Is taken in, forgive our noises

And teach us our recollections: to throw away
    The tiniest fault of someone we love
Is out of the question, says Aphrodite,
    Who should know, yet one has known people

Who have done just that. Approachable as you seem,
 I dare not ask you if you bless the poets,
For you do not look as if you ever read them,
 Nor can I see a reason why you should.

The Love Feast

In an upper room at midnight
See us gathered on behalf
Of love according to the gospel
Of the radio-phonograph.

Lou is telling Anne what Molly
Said to Mark behind her back;
Jack likes Jill who worships George
Who has the hots for Jack.

Catechumens make their entrance;
Steep enthusiastic eyes
Flicker after tits and baskets;
Someone vomits; someone cries.

Willy cannot bear his father,
Lilian is afraid of kids;
The Love that rules the sun and stars
Permits what He forbids.

Adrian's pleasure-loving dachshund
In a sinner's lap lies curled;
Drunken absent-minded fingers
Pat a sinless world.

Who is Jenny lying to
In her call, Collect, to Rome?
The Love that made her out of nothing
Tells me to go home.

But that Miss Number in the corner
Playing hard to get....
I am sorry I'm not sorry...
Make me chaste, Lord, but not yet.

The Chimeras

Absence of heart — as in public buildings —
Absence of mind — as in public speeches —
Absence of worth — as in goods intended for the public,

Are telltale signs that a chimera has just dined
On someone else; of him, poor foolish fellow,
Not a scrap is left, not even his name.

Indescribable — being neither this nor that —
Uncountable — being any number —
Unreal — being anything but what they are,

And ugly customers for someone to encounter,
It is our fault entirely if we do:
They cannot touch us; it is we who will touch them.

Curious from wantonness — to see what they are like —
Cruel from fear — to put a stop to them —
Incredulous from conceit — to prove they cannot be —

We prod or kick or measure and are lost:
The stronger we are the sooner all is over;
It is our strength with which they gobble us up.

If someone, being chaste, brave, humble,
Get by them safely, he is still in danger,
With pity remembering what once they were,

Of turning back to help them. Don't.
What they were once was what they would not be;
Not liking what they are not is what now they are.

No one can help them; walk on, keep on walking,
And do not let your goodness self-deceive you:
It is good that they are but not that they are thus.

Merax & Mullin

There is one devil in the lexicon
Who waits for those who would unwish themselves
Yet blow a trumpet,
To fill their voids of insufficiency
With pejorative noises.

In timid, gouty, bastard, cuckolded fingers
How swift, so prompted, fly polemic pens,
Scoring the foolscap
With bestial engagements quite unknown
To Natural History,

And when superior devils start a war,
How soon the home-sick ranks in either army
Credit his cosmos,
Where officers, machinery, abstractions
Are sexually aberrant.

There is an even nastier, more deadly,
Philological imp,
Who with endearing diminutives eggs on
Laodicean lovers till they swear
Undying love.

Limbo Culture

The tribes of Limbo, travellers report,
On first encounter seem much like ourselves;
They keep their houses practically clean,
Their watches round about a standard time,
They serve you almost appetising meals:
But no one says he saw a Limbo child.

The language spoken by the tribes of Limbo
Has many words far subtler than our own

To indicate how much, how little, something
Is pretty closely or not quite the case,
But none you could translate by *Yes* or *No*,
Nor do its pronouns distinguish between Persons.

In tales related by the tribes of Limbo,
Dragon and Knight set to with fang and sword
But miss their rival always by a hair's-breadth,
Old Crone and Stripling pass a crucial point,
She seconds early and He seconds late,
A magic purse mistakes the legal tender:

'And so,' runs their concluding formula,
'Prince and Princess are nearly married still.'
Why this concern, so marked in Limbo culture,
This love for inexactness? Could it be
A Limbo tribesman only loves himself?
For that, we know, cannot be done exactly.

There Will Be No Peace

Though mild clear weather
Smile again on the shire of your esteem
And its colours come back, the storm has changed you:
    You will not forget, ever,
The darkness blotting out hope, the gale
    Prophesying your downfall.

You must live with your knowledge.
Way back, beyond, outside of you are others,
In moonless absences you never heard of,
    Who have certainly heard of you,
Beings of unknown number and gender:
    And they do not like you.

What have you done to them?
Nothing? Nothing is not an answer:

You will come to believe — how can you help it? —
    That you did, you did do something;
You will find yourself wishing you could make them laugh,
    You will long for their friendship.

    There will be no peace.
Fight back, then, with such courage as you have
And every unchivalrous dodge you know of,
    Clear in your conscience on this:
Their cause, if they had one, is nothing to them now;
    They hate for hate's sake.

A Household

When, to disarm suspicious minds at lunch
Before coming to the point, or at golf,
The bargain driven, to soothe hurt feelings,

He talks about his home, he never speaks
(A reticence for which they all admire him)
Of his bride so worshipped and so early lost,

But proudly tells of that young scamp his heir,
Of black eyes given and received, thrashings
Endured without a sound to save a chum;

Or calls their spotted maleness to revere
His saintly mother, calm and kind and wise,
A grand old lady pouring out the tea.

Whom, though, has he ever asked for the week-end?
Out to his country mansion in the evening,
Another merger signed, he drives alone:

To be avoided by a miserable runt
Who wets his bed and cannot throw or whistle,
A tell-tale, a crybaby, a failure;

To the revilings of a slatternly hag
Who caches bottles in her mattress, spits
And shouts obscenities from the landing;

Worse, to find both in an unholy alliance,
Youth stealing Age the liquor-cupboard key,
Age teaching Youth to lie with a straight face.

Disgraces to keep hidden from the world
Where rivals, envying his energy and brains
And with rattling skeletons of their own,

Would see in him the villain of this household,
Whose bull-voice scared a sensitive young child,
Whose coldness drove a doting parent mad.

Besides, (which might explain why he has neither
Altered his will nor called the doctor in)
He half believes, call it a superstition,

It is for his sake that they hate and fear him:
Should they unmask and show themselves worth loving,
Loving and sane and manly, he would die.

'The Truest Poetry is the most Feigning'

(For Edgar Wind)

By all means sing of love but, if you do,
Please make a rare old proper hullabaloo:
When ladies ask *How much do you love me?*
The Christian answer is *così-così*;
But poets are not celibate divines:
Had Dante said so, who would read his lines?
Be subtle, various, ornamental, clever,
And do not listen to those critics ever
Whose crude provincial gullets crave in books
Plain cooking made still plainer by plain cooks,

As though the Muse preferred her half-wit sons;
Good poets have a weakness for bad puns.

Suppose your Beatrice be, as usual, late,
And you would tell us how it feels to wait,
You're free to think, what may be even true,
You're so in love that one hour seems like two,
But write — *As I sat waiting for her call,*
Each second longer darker seemed than all
(Something like this but more elaborate still)
Those raining centuries it took to fill
That quarry whence Endymion's Love was torn;
From such ingenious fibs are poems born.
Then, should she leave you for some other guy,
Or ruin you with debts, or go and die,
No metaphor, remember, can express
A real historical unhappiness;
Your tears have value if they make us gay;
O *Happy Grief!* is all sad verse can say.

The living girl's your business (some odd sorts
Have been an inspiration to men's thoughts):
Yours may be old enough to be your mother,
Or have one leg that's shorter than the other,
Or play Lacrosse or do the Modern Dance,
To you that's destiny, to us it's chance;
We cannot love your love till she take on,
Through you, the wonders of a paragon.
Sing her triumphant passage to our land,
The sun her footstool, the moon in her right hand,
And seven planets blazing in her hair,
Queen of the Night and Empress of the Air;
Tell how her fleet by nine king swans is led,
Wild geese write magic letters overhead
And hippocampi follow in her wake
With Amphisboene, gentle for her sake;
Sing her descent on the exulting shore
To bless the vines and put an end to war.

If half-way through such praises of your dear,
Riot and shooting fill the streets with fear,
And overnight as in some terror dream
Poets are suspect with the New Regime,
Stick at your desk and hold your panic in,
What you are writing may still save your skin:
Re-sex the pronouns, add a few details,
And, lo, a panegyric ode which hails
(How is the Censor, bless his heart, to know?)
The new pot-bellied Generalissimo.
Some epithets, of course, like *lily-breasted*
Need modifying to, say, *lion-chested*,
A title *Goddess of wry-necks and wrens*
To *Great Reticulator of the fens*,
But in an hour your poem qualifies
For a State pension or His annual prize,
And you will die in bed (which He will not:
That public nuisance will be hanged or shot).
Though honest Iagos, true to form, will write
Shame! in your margins, *Toady! Hypocrite!*
True hearts, clear heads will hear the note of glory
And put inverted commas round the story,
Thinking — *Old Sly-boots! We shall never know
Her name or nature. Well, it's better so.*

For given Man, by birth, by education,
Imago Dei who forgot his station,
The self-made creature who himself unmakes,
The only creature ever made who fakes,
With no more nature in his loving smile
Than in his theories of a natural style,
What but tall tales, the luck of verbal playing,
Can trick his lying nature into saying
That love, or truth in any serious sense,
Like orthodoxy, is a reticence?

We Too Had Known Golden Hours

We, too, had known golden hours
When body and soul were in tune,
Had danced with our true loves
By the light of a full moon,
And sat with the wise and good
As tongues grew witty and gay
Over some noble dish
Out of Escoffier;
Had felt the intrusive glory
Which tears reserve apart,
And would in the old grand manner
Have sung from a resonant heart.
But, pawed-at and gossiped-over
By the promiscuous crowd,
Concocted by editors
Into spells to befuddle the crowd,
All words like Peace and Love,
All sane affirmative speech,
Had been soiled, profaned, debased
To a horrid mechanical screech.
No civil style survived
That pandaemonium
But the wry, the sotto-voce,
Ironic and monochrome:
And where should we find shelter
For joy or mere content
When little was left standing
But the suburb of dissent?

Secrets

That we are always glad
When the Ugly Princess, parting the bushes
To find out why the woodcutter's children are happy,
Disturbs a hornets' nest, that we feel no pity

When the informer is trapped by the gang in a steam-room,
That we howl with joy
When the short-sighted Professor of Icelandic
Pronounces the Greek inscription
A Runic riddle which he then translates:

Denouncing by proxy our commonest fault as our worst;
That, waiting in his room for a friend,
We start so soon to turn over his letters,
That with such assurance we repeat as our own
Another's story, that, dear me, how often
We kiss in order to tell,
Defines precisely what we mean by love: —
To share a secret.

The joke, which we seldom see, is on us;
For only true hearts know how little it matters
What the secret is they keep:
An old, a new, a blue, a borrowed something,
Anything will do for children
Made in God's image and therefore
Not like the others, not like our dear dumb friends
Who, poor things, have nothing to hide,
Not, thank God, like our Father either
From whom no secrets are hid.

Numbers and Faces

The Kingdom of Number is all boundaries
Which may be beautiful and must be true;
To ask if it is big or small proclaims one
The sort of lover who should stick to faces.

Lovers of small numbers go benignly potty,
Believe all tales are thirteen chapters long,
Have animal doubles, carry pentagrams,
Are Millerites, Baconians, Flat-Earth-Men.

Lovers of big numbers go horridly mad,
Would have the Swiss abolished, all of us
Well purged, somatotyped, baptised, taught baseball:
They empty bars, spoil parties, run for Congress.

True, between faces almost any number
Might come in handy, and One is always real;
But which could any face call good, for calling
Infinity a number does not make it one.

Objects

All that which lies outside our sort of why,
Those wordless creatures who are there as well,
Remote from mourning yet in sight and cry,
Make time more golden than we meant to tell.

Tearless, their surfaces appear as deep
As any longing we believe we had;
If shapes can so to their own edges keep,
No separation proves a being bad.

There is less grief than wonder on the whole,
Even at sunset, though of course we care
Each time the same old shadow falls across

One Person who is not: somewhere, a soul,
Light in her bestial substance, well aware,
Extols the silence of how soon a loss.

Words

A sentence uttered makes a world appear
Where all things happen as it says they do;
We doubt the speaker, not the tongue we hear:
Words have no word for words that are not true.

Syntactically, though, it must be clear;
One cannot change the subject half-way through,
Nor alter tenses to appease the ear:
Arcadian tales are hard-luck stories too.

But should we want to gossip all the time,
Were fact not fiction for us at its best,
Or find a charm in syllables that rhyme,

Were not our fate by verbal chance expressed,
As rustics in a ring-dance pantomime
The Knight at some lone cross-roads of his quest?

The Song

So large a morning so itself to lean
Over so many and such little hills
All at rest in roundness and rigs of green
Can cope with a rebellious wing that wills
To better its obedient double quite
As daring in the lap of any lake
The wind from which ascension puts to flight
Tribes of a beauty which no care can break.

Climbing to song it hopes to make amends
For whiteness drabbed for glory said away
And be immortal after but because
Light upon a valley where its love was
So lacks all picture of reproach it ends
Denying what it started up to say.

One Circumlocution

Sometimes we see astonishingly clearly
The out-there-now we are already in;
Now that is not what we are here-for really.

All its to-do is bound to re-occur,
Is nothing therefore that we need to say;
How then to make its compromise refer

To what could not be otherwise instead
And has its being as its own to be,
The once-for-all that is not seen nor said?

Tell for the power how to thunderclaps
The graves flew open, the rivers ran up-hill;
Such staged importance is at most perhaps.

Speak well of moonlight on a winding stair,
Of light-boned children under great green oaks:
The wonder, yes, but death should not be there.

One circumlocution as used as any
Depends, it seems, upon the joke of rhyme
For the pure joy; else why should so many

Poems which make us cry direct us to
Ourselves at our least apt, least kind, least true,
Where a blank I loves blankly a blank You?

Horae Canonicae

('*Immolatus vicerit*')

1. PRIME

Simultaneously, as soundlessly,
   Spontaneously, suddenly
As, at the vaunt of the dawn, the kind
   Gates of the body fly open
To its world beyond, the gates of the mind,
   The horn gate and the ivory gate
Swing to, swing shut, instantaneously
   Quell the nocturnal rummage
Of its rebellious fronde, ill-favoured,
   Ill-natured and second-rate,
Disenfranchised, widowed and orphaned
   By an historical mistake:
Recalled from the shades to be a seeing being,
   From absence to be on display,
Without a name or history I wake
   Between my body and the day.

Holy this moment, wholly in the right,
   As, in complete obedience
To the light's laconic outcry, next
   As a sheet, near as a wall,
Out there as a mountain's poise of stone,
   The world is present, about,
And I know that I am, here, not alone
   But with a world and rejoice
Unvexed, for the will has still to claim
   This adjacent arm as my own,
The memory to name me, resume
   Its routine of praise and blame,
And smiling to me is this instant while
   Still the day is intact, and I
The Adam sinless in our beginning,
   Adam still previous to any act.

I draw breath; that is of course to wish
    No matter what, to be wise,
To be different, to die and the cost,
    No matter how, is Paradise
Lost of course and myself owing a death:
    The eager ridge, the steady sea,
The flat roofs of the fishing village
    Still asleep in its bunny,
Though as fresh and sunny still are not friends
    But things to hand, this ready flesh
No honest equal, but my accomplice now,
    My assassin to be, and my name
Stands for my historical share of care
    For a lying self-made city,
Afraid of our living task, the dying
    Which the coming day will ask.

2. TERCE

    After shaking paws with his dog
(Whose bark would tell the world that he is always kind),
    The hangman sets off briskly over the heath;
He does not know yet who will be provided
    To do the high works of Justice with:
Gently closing the door of his wife's bedroom
    (Today she has one of her headaches),
With a sigh the judge descends his marble stair;
    He does not know by what sentence
He will apply on earth the Law that rules the stars:
    And the poet, taking a breather
Round his garden before starting his eclogue,
    Does not know whose Truth he will tell.

    Sprites of hearth and store-room, godlings
Of professional mysteries, the Big Ones
    Who can annihilate a city
Cannot be bothered with this moment: we are left,
    Each to his secret cult. Now each of us

Prays to an image of his image of himself;
   'Let me get through this coming day
Without a dressing down from a superior,
   Being worsted in a repartee,
Or behaving like an ass in front of the girls;
   Let something exciting happen,
Let me find a lucky coin on a sidewalk.
   Let me hear a new funny story.'

   At this hour we all might be anyone:
It is only our victim who is without a wish
   Who knows already (that is what
We can never forgive. If he knows the answers,
   Then why are we here, why is there even dust?),
Knows already that, in fact, our prayers are heard,
   That not one of us will slip up,
That the machinery of our world will function
   Without a hitch, that today, for once,
There will be no squabbling on Mount Olympus,
   No Chthonian mutters of unrest,
But no other miracle, knows that by sundown
   We shall have had a good Friday.

3. SEXT

I

You need not see what someone is doing
to know if it is his vocation,

you have only to watch his eyes:
a cook mixing a sauce, a surgeon

making a primary incision,
a clerk completing a bill of lading,

wear the same rapt expression,
forgetting themselves in a function.

How beautiful it is,
that eye-on-the-object look.

To ignore the appetitive goddesses,
to desert the formidable shrines

of Rhea, Aphrodite, Demeter, Diana,
to pray instead to St. Phocas,

St. Barbara, San Saturnino,
or whoever one's patron is,

that one may be worthy of their mystery,
what a prodigious step to have taken.

There should be monuments, there should be odes,
to the nameless heroes who took it first,

to the first flaker of flints
who forgot his dinner,

the first collector of sea-shells
to remain celibate.

Where should we be but for them?
Feral still, un-housetrained, still

wandering through forests without
a consonant to our names,

slaves of Dame Kind, lacking
all notion of a city,

and, at this noon, for this death,
there would be no agents.

II

You need not hear what orders he is giving
to know if someone has authority,

you have only to watch his mouth:
when a besieging general sees

a city wall breached by his troops,
when a bacteriologist

realizes in a flash what was wrong
with his hypothesis, when,

from a glance at the jury, the prosecutor,
knows the defendant will hang,

their lips and the lines around them
relax, assuming an expression

not of simple pleasure at getting
their own sweet way but of satisfaction

at being right, an incarnation
of *Fortitudo, Justicia, Nous.*

You may not like them much
(Who does?) but we owe them

basilicas, divas,
dictionaries, pastoral verse,

the courtesies of the city:
without these judicial mouths

(which belong for the most part
to very great scoundrels)

how squalid existence would be,
tethered for life to some hut village,

afraid of the local snake
or the local ford demon,

speaking the local patois
of some three hundred words

(think of the family squabbles and the
poison-pens, think of the inbreeding),

and, at this noon, there would be no authority
to command this death.

III

Anywhere you like, somewhere
on broad-chested life-giving Earth,

anywhere between her thirstlands
and undrinkable Ocean,

the crowd stands perfectly still,
its eyes (which seem one) and its mouths

(which seem infinitely many)
expressionless, perfectly blank.

The crowd does not see (what everyone sees)
a boxing match, a train wreck,

a battleship being launched,
does not wonder (as everyone wonders)

who will win, what flag she will fly,
how many will be burned alive,

is never distracted
(as everyone is always distracted)

by a barking dog, a smell of fish,
a mosquito on a bald head:

the crowd sees only one thing
(which only the crowd can see),

an epiphany of that
which does whatever is done.

Whatever god a person believes in,
in whatever way he believes

(no two are exactly alike),
as one of the crowd he believes

and only believes in that
in which there is only one way of believing.

Few people accept each other and most
will never do anything properly,

but the crowd rejects no one, joining the crowd
is the only thing all men can do.

Only because of that can we say
all men are our brothers,

superior, because of that,
to the social exoskeletons: When

have they ever ignored their queens,
for one second stopped work

on their provincial cities, to worship
The Prince of this world like us,

at this noon, on this hill,
in the occasion of this dying?

4. NONES

What we know to be not possible,
  Though time after time foretold
By wild hermits, by shaman and sybil
  Gibbering in their trances,
Or revealed to a child in some chance rhyme
  Like *will* and *kill*, comes to pass
Before we realize it. We are surprised
  At the ease and speed of our deed
And uneasy: It is barely three,
  Mid-afternoon, yet the blood
Of our sacrifice is already
  Dry on the grass; we are not prepared
For silence so sudden and so soon;
  The day is too hot, too bright, too still,
Too ever, the dead remains too nothing.
  What shall we do till nightfall?

The wind has dropped and we have lost our public.
  The faceless many who always
Collect when any world is to be wrecked,
  Blown up, burnt down, cracked open,
Felled, sawn in two, hacked through, torn apart,
  Have all melted away. Not one
Of these who in the shade of walls and trees
  Lie sprawled now, calmly sleeping,
Harmless as sheep, can remember why
  He shouted or what about
So loudly in the sunshine this morning;
  All if challenged would reply
— 'It was a monster with one red eye,
  A crowd that saw him die, not I.' —
The hangman has gone to wash, the soldiers to eat:
  We are left alone with our feat.

The Madonna with the green woodpecker,
  The Madonna of the fig-tree,
The Madonna beside the yellow dam,
  Turn their kind faces from us

And our projects under construction,
　　Look only in one direction,
Fix their gaze on our completed work:
　　Pile-driver, concrete-mixer,
Crane and pick-axe wait to be used again,
　　But how can we repeat this?
Outliving our act, we stand where we are,
　　As disregarded as some
Discarded artifact of our own,
　　Like torn gloves, rusted kettles,
Abandoned branch-lines, worn lop-sided
　　Grindstones buried in nettles.

This mutilated flesh, our victim,
　　Explains too nakedly, too well,
The spell of the asparagus garden,
　　The aim of our chalk-pit game; stamps,
Birds' eggs are not the same, behind the wonder
　　Of tow-paths and sunken lanes,
Behind the rapture on the spiral stair,
　　We shall always now be aware
Of the deed into which they lead, under
　　The mock chase and mock capture,
The racing and tussling and splashing,
　　The panting and the laughter,
Be listening for the cry and stillness
　　To follow after: wherever
The sun shines, brooks run, books are written,
　　There will also be this death.

Soon cool tramontana will stir the leaves,
　　The shops will re-open at four,
The empty blue bus in the empty pink square
　　Fill up and depart: we have time
To misrepresent, excuse, deny,
　　Mythify, use this event
While, under a hotel bed, in prison,
　　Down wrong turnings, its meaning

Waits for our lives. Sooner than we would choose
   Bread will melt, water will burn,
And the great quell begin, Abaddon
   Set up his triple gallows
At our seven gates, fat Belial make
   Our wives waltz naked; meanwhile
It would be best to go home, if we have a home,
   In any case good to rest.

That our dreaming wills may seem to escape
   This dead calm, wander instead
On knife edges, on black and white squares,
   Across moss, baize, velvet, boards,
Over cracks and hillocks, in mazes
   Of string and penitent cones,
Down granite ramps and damp passages,
   Through gates that will not relatch
And doors marked *Private*, pursued by Moors
   And watched by latent robbers,
To hostile villages at the heads of fjords,
   To dark chateaux where wind sobs
In the pine-trees and telephones ring,
   Inviting trouble, to a room,
Lit by one weak bulb, where our Double sits
   Writing and does not look up.

That, while we are thus away, our own wronged flesh
   May work undisturbed, restoring
The order we try to destroy, the rhythm
   We spoil out of spite: valves close
And open exactly, glands secrete,
   Vessels contract and expand
At the right moment, essential fluids
   Flow to renew exhausted cells,
Not knowing quite what has happened, but awed
   By death like all the creatures
Now watching this spot, like the hawk looking down
   Without blinking, the smug hens

Passing close by in their pecking order,
   The bug whose view is balked by grass,
Or the deer who shyly from afar
   Peer through chinks in the forest.

5. VESPERS

If the hill overlooking our city has always been known as
Adam's Grave, only at dusk can you see the recumbent giant, his
head turned to the west, his right arm resting for ever on Eve's
haunch,

can you learn, from the way he looks up at the scandalous pair,
what a citizen really thinks of his citizenship,

just as now you can hear in a drunkard's caterwaul his rebel
sorrows crying for a parental discipline, in lustful eyes perceive a
disconsolate soul,

scanning with desperation all passing limbs for some vestige of
her faceless angel who in that long ago when wishing was a help
mounted her once and vanished:

For Sun and Moon supply their conforming masks, but in this
hour of civil twilight all must wear their own faces.

And it is now that our two paths cross.

Both simultaneously recognise his Anti-type: that I am an
Arcadian, that he is a Utopian.

He notes, with contempt, my Aquarian belly: I note, with
alarm, his Scorpion's mouth.

He would like to see me cleaning latrines: I would like to see
him removed to some other planet.

Neither speaks. What experience could we possibly share?

Glancing at a lampshade in a store window, I observe it is too hideous for anyone in their senses to buy: He observes it is too expensive for a peasant to buy.

Passing a slum child with rickets, I look the other way: He looks the other way if he passes a chubby one.

I hope our senators will behave like saints, provided they don't reform me: He hopes they will behave like *baritoni cattivi*, and, when lights burn late in the Citadel,

I (who have never seen the inside of a police station) am shocked and think, 'Were the city as free as they say, after sundown all her bureaus would be huge black stones.':

He (who has been beaten up several times) is not shocked at all but thinks, 'One fine night our boys will be working up there.'

You can see, then, why, between my Eden and his New Jerusalem, no treaty is negotiable.

In my Eden a person who dislikes Bellini has the good manners not to get born: In his New Jerusalem a person who dislikes work will be very sorry he was born.

In my Eden we have a few beam-engines, saddle-tank loco-motives, overshot waterwheels and other beautiful pieces of obsolete machinery to play with: In his New Jerusalem even chefs will be cucumber-cool machine minders.

In my Eden our only source of political news is gossip: In his New Jerusalem there will be a special daily in simplified spelling for non-verbal types.

In my Eden each observes his compulsive rituals and superstitious tabus but we have no morals: In his New Jerusalem the temples will be empty but all will practise the rational virtues.

One reason for his contempt is that I have only to close my eyes, cross the iron footbridge to the tow-path, take the barge through the short brick tunnel and

there I stand in Eden again, welcomed back by the krum-horns, doppions, sordumes of jolly miners and a bob major from the Cathedral (romanesque) of St. Sophie (*Die Kalte*):

One reason for my alarm is that, when he closes his eyes, he arrives, not in New Jerusalem, but on some august day of outrage when hellikins cavort through ruined drawing-rooms and fish-wives intervene in the Chamber or

some autumn night of delations and noyades, when the un-repentant thieves (including me) are sequestered and those he hates shall hate themselves instead.

So with a passing glance we take the other's posture. Already our steps recede, heading, incorrigible each, towards his kind of meal and evening.

Was it (as it must look to any god of cross-roads) simply a fortuitous intersection of life-paths, loyal to different fibs?

Or also a rendezvous between two accomplices who, in spite of themselves, cannot resist meeting

to remind the other (do both, at bottom, desire truth?) of that half of their secret which he would most like to forget,

forcing us both, for a fraction of a second, to remember our victim (but for him I could forget the blood, but for me he could forget the innocence),

on whose immolation (call him Abel, Remus, whom you will, it is one Sin Offering) arcadias, utopias, our dear old bag of a democracy are alike founded:

For without a cement of blood (it must be human, it must be innocent) no secular wall will safely stand.

6. COMPLINE

Now, as desire and the things desired
    Cease to require attention,
As, seizing its chance, the body escapes,
    Section by section, to join
Plants in their chaster peace which is more
    To its real taste, now a day is its past,
Its last deed and feeling in, should come
    The instant of recollection
When the whole thing makes sense: it comes, but all
    I recall are doors banging,
Two housewives scolding, an old man gobbling,
    A child's wild look of envy,
Actions, words, that could fit any tale,
    And I fail to see either plot
Or meaning; I cannot remember
    A thing between noon and three.

Nothing is with me now but a sound,
    A heart's rhythm, a sense of stars
Leisurely walking around, and both
    Talk a language of motion
I can measure but not read: maybe
    My heart is confessing her part
In what happened to us from noon till three,
    That constellations indeed
Sing of some hilarity beyond
    All liking and happening,
But, knowing I neither know what they know
    Nor what I ought to know, scorning
All vain fornications of fancy,
    Now let me, blessing them both
For the sweetness of their cassations,
    Accept our separations.

A stride from now will take me into dream,
    Leave me, without a status,
Among its unwashed tribes of wishes
    Who have no dances and no jokes

But a magic cult to propitiate
    What happens from noon till three,
Odd rites which they hide from me — should I chance,
    Say, on youths in an oak-wood
Insulting a white deer, bribes nor threats
    Will get them to blab, and then,
Past untruth is one step to nothing,
    For the end, for me as for cities,
Is total absence: what comes to be
    Must go back into non-being
For the sake of the equity, the rhythm
    Past measure or comprehending.

Can poets (can men in television)
    Be saved? It is not easy
To believe in unknowable justice
    Or pray in the name of a love
Whose name one's forgotten: *libera*
    Me, libera C (dear C)
And all poor s-o-b's who never
    Do anything properly, spare
Us in the youngest day when all are
    Shaken awake, facts are facts,
(And I shall know exactly what happened
    Today between noon and three)
That we, too, may come to the picnic
    With nothing to hide, join the dance
As it moves in perichoresis,
    Turns about the abiding tree.

7. LAUDS

Among the leaves the small birds sing;
The crow of the cock commands awaking:
In solitude, for company.

Bright shines the sun on creatures mortal;
Men of their neighbours become sensible:
In solitude, for company.

The crow of the cock commands awaking;
Already the mass-bell goes dong-ding:
In solitude, for company.

Men of their neighbours become sensible;
God bless the Realm, God bless the People:
In solitude, for company.

Already the mass-bell goes dong-ding;
The dripping mill-wheel is again turning:
In solitude, for company.

God bless the Realm, God bless the People;
God bless this green world temporal:
In solitude, for company.

The dripping mill-wheel is again turning;
Among the leaves the small birds sing:
In solitude, for company.

Good-Bye to the Mezzogiorno

(For Carlo Izzo)

Out of a gothic North, the pallid children
    Of a potato, beer-or-whisky
Guilt culture, we behave like our fathers and come
    Southward into a sunburnt otherwhere

Of vineyards, baroque, *la bella figura,*
    To these feminine townships where men
Are males, and siblings untrained in a ruthless
    Verbal in-fighting as it is taught

In Protestant rectories upon drizzling
    Sunday afternoons — no more as unwashed
Barbarians out for gold, nor as profiteers
    Hot for Old Masters, but for plunder

338

Nevertheless — some believing *amore*
    Is better down South and much cheaper
(Which is doubtful), some persuaded exposure
    To strong sunlight is lethal to germs

(Which is patently false) and others, like me,
    In middle-age hoping to twig from
What we are not what we might be next, a question
    The South seems never to raise. Perhaps

A tongue in which Nestor and Apemantus,
    Don Ottavio and Don Giovanni make
Equally beautiful sounds is unequipped
    To frame it, or perhaps in this heat

It is nonsense: the Myth of an Open Road
    Which runs past the orchard gate and beckons
Three brothers in turn to set out over the hills
    And far away, is an invention

Of a climate where it is a pleasure to walk
    And a landscape less populated
Than this one. Even so, to us it looks very odd
    Never to see an only child engrossed

In a game it has made up, a pair of friends
    Making fun in a private lingo,
Or a body sauntering by himself who is not
    Wanting, even as it perplexes

Our ears when cats are called *Cat* and dogs either
    Lupo, *Nero* or *Bobby*. Their dining
Puts us to shame: we can only envy a people
    So frugal by nature it costs them

No effort not to guzzle and swill. Yet (if I
    Read their faces rightly after ten years)
They are without hope. The Greeks used to call the Sun
    He-who-smites-from-afar, and from here, where

Shadows are dagger-edged, the daily ocean blue,
    I can see what they meant: his unwinking
Outrageous eye laughs to scorn any notion
    Of change or escape, and a silent

Ex-volcano, without a stream or a bird,
    Echoes that laugh. This could be a reason
Why they take the silencers off their Vespas,
    Turn their radios up to full volume,

And a minim saint can expect rockets — noise
    As a counter-magic, a way of saying
Boo to the Three Sisters: 'Mortal we may be,
    But we are still here!' — might cause them to hanker

After proximities — in streets packed solid
    With human flesh, their souls feel immune
To all metaphysical threats. We are rather shocked,
    But we need shocking: to accept space, to own

That surfaces need not be superficial
    Nor gestures vulgar, cannot really
Be taught within earshot of running water
    Or in sight of a cloud. As pupils

We are not bad, but hopeless as tutors: Goethe,
    Tapping homeric hexameters
On the shoulder-blade of a Roman girl, is
    (I wish it were someone else) the figure

Of all our stamp: no doubt he treated her well,
    But one would draw the line at calling
The Helena begotten on that occasion,
    Queen of his Second *Walpurgisnacht*,

Her baby: between those who mean by a life a
    Bildungsroman and those to whom living
Means to-be-visible-now, there yawns a gulf
    Embraces cannot bridge. If we try

To 'go southern', we spoil in no time, we grow
   Flabby, dingily lecherous, and
Forget to pay bills: that no one has heard of them
   Taking the Pledge or turning to Yoga

Is a comforting thought — in that case, for all
   The spiritual loot we tuck away,
We do them no harm — and entitles us, I think
   To one little scream at *A piacere*,

Not two. Go I must, but I go grateful (even
   To a certain *Monte*) and invoking
My sacred meridian names, *Vico, Verga,*
   Pirandello, Bernini, Bellini,

To bless this region, its vendanges, and those
   Who call it home: though one cannot always
Remember exactly why one has been happy,
   There is no forgetting that one was.

Index of First Lines

344

345

349

Wystan Hugh Auden

was born in York, England, in 1907. He has been a resident of the United States since 1939, and an American citizen since 1946. Educated at Gresham's School, Holt, and at Christ Church, Oxford, he became associated with a small group of young writers in London—among them Stephen Spender and Christopher Isherwood—who became recognized as the most promising of the new generation in English letters. He collaborated with Isherwood on several plays, among them *The Dog Beneath the Skin* and *The Ascent of F-6* (available as *Two Great Plays* in Vintage Books).

Mr. Auden is the author of several volumes of poetry, including *About the House, Homage to Clio, The Double Man, For the Time Being, The Age of Anxiety, Nones,* and *The Shield of Achilles.* His *Selected Poetry* appears in The Modern Library. *The Enchafèd Flood,* three critical essays on the romantic spirit, is available in Vintage Books. A volume of essays, *The Dyer's Hand,* appeared in 1962. A new edition of *The Orators* was published in 1967.

Mr. Auden has been the recipient of a number of awards, among them the Pulitzer Prize, the National Book Award, the Bollingen Prize for Poetry, the Guinness Poetry Award and, in 1967, the National Medal for Literature given by the National Book Committee.